Healing Through Nature:
Mindful Practices for Emotional Healing

By Edward Chalk

Healing Through Nature: Mindful Practices for Emotional Healing

Edward Chalk

Copyright © 2024 Edward Chalk

All rights reserved. No part of this book may be reproduced in any form or by any electronic or mechanical means, including information storage and retrieval systems, without permission in writing from the author, except by a reviewer who may quote brief passages in a review.

ISBN: 9798328010696

First published June 2024

Library of Congress Cataloguing-in-Publication Data

Chalk, Edward
Healing Through Nature: Mindful Practices for Emotional Healing
Edward Chalk

1. Self-Help. 2. Mindfulness. 3. Emotional Healing.
   Library of Congress Classification: BF637.S4
   Dewey Decimal Classification: 158.1

For more information, please contact:

Edward Chalk
Email: edward@fleetingswallow.com

Published by Fleeting Swallow Press

Contents

- Introduction 8
  - Always Busy 8
  - Nature as a Guide 8
  - Conclusion 9
- Section I: The Problem with Modernity 10
- Chapter 1. The Industrial Revolution 11
- Chapter 2. Beyond Luxury Retreats 14
  - The Importance of Immersion 14
  - Conclusion 15
- Chapter 3. The Machine 16
  - The Rise of the Machine 17
  - Mindful Practices for Reconnecting 18
  - Conclusion 19
- Section II. Natural Being 20
- Chapter 4. Hyperthinking 21
  - Thinking Too Much 21
  - Robust Thinking 22
  - Mindfulness Exercises for Robust Thinking 22
  - Conclusion 23
- Chapter 5. Complexity 24
  - The Maze of Life 24
  - Clarity through Nature 25
  - Mindfulness Exercises for Navigating Complexity 26
  - Conclusion 27
- Chapter 6: Distraction 28
  - Self-Possession 29
  - Mindfulness Exercises 29
  - Conclusion 31
- Chapter 7: Professionalism 32

- The Weight of Expectations 32
- The Pressure of the Facade 33
- Strength of Character 33
- Reimagining Ourselves Through Mindfulness 34
- Conclusion 35

Chapter 8. Information Overload 36
- Understanding Information Overload 36
- The Brain's Processing Power 36
- Nature as an Antidote to Information Overload 37
- Mindfulness Exercises for Overcoming Information Overload 37
- Conclusion 38

Chapter 9. The Need to Own 39
- *Joie de Vivre*: The Joy of Living 39
- Mindfulness Exercises for Embracing Simplicity 40
- Returning to Civilization 42
- Conclusion 42

Section III: Self 43

Chapter 11. Peace of Mind 44
- Understanding Peace of Mind 44
- How We Lose Peace of Mind 45
- Making a Conscious Decision to Regain Peace of Mind 45
- Practical Steps to Find Peace in Nature 45
- Mindfulness Exercises in Nature 46
- Conclusion 47

Chapter 12. Solitude 48
- How to Practice Solitude in Nature 48
- Conclusion 49

Chapter 13. Words 50
- The Wordless Inner Self 50
- Words and the Modern World 50

    The Wordlessness of Nature 51
    Mindfulness Exercises for Wordlessness 51
    Conclusion 52

Chapter 14. Our Whole Selves 53
    The Bits of Self We Leave Behind 54
    Nature as a Catalyst for Rediscovery 55
    Conclusion 56

Chapter 15. The Natural Healing Ability of the Mind 57
    Understanding the Mind's Healing Potential 57
    Mindful Practices for Encouraging Natural Healing 58
    Conclusion 59

Section III: The Health of the Natural World 60

Chapter 17. Earth: The Richness of the Soil 61
    The Importance of Soil 61
    The Formation of Soil 62
    Connecting to the Soil 63
    Conclusion 65

Chapter 18. Fire: The Wonder of Sunlight 66
    The Lifeblood of Nature 67
    Photosynthesis and Global Warming 67
    Mindfulness Exercises 68
    Conclusion 69

Chapter 19. Water: Rain and Renewal 70
    The Life-Giving Power of Rain 70
    The Role of Clouds 71
    Mindfulness Exercises for Connecting with Rain 72
    Conclusion 73

Chapter 20. Wind: The Breath of Life 74
    The Vital Role of Wind 74
    Forms of Wind 75

    Mindfulness Exercises for Connecting with the Wind 75

    Conclusion 77

Section IV: The Five Senses 78

Chapter 21. Introduction: Sensory Healing 79

Chapter 22. Smell 81

    The Olfactory Journey: From Nose to Memory 81

    The Emotional Landscape of Smell 82

    The Modern Challenge: Smell in Urban Environments 82

    Cultivating a Deeper Connection with Smell 82

    Conclusion 83

Chapter 23. Bringing Aromatic Nature Indoors 84

    Creating a Scent Garden 86

Chapter 24. Touch 87

    The Journey of Touch: From Skin to Brain 87

    The Emotional Landscape of Touch 87

    The Timelessness of Touch 88

    The Role of Touch in Daily Life 88

    The Modern Challenge: Touch in Urban Environments 89

    Cultivating a Deeper Connection with Touch 89

    Conclusion 89

Chapter 25. Engaging with Nature Through Texture 90

    Textured Plants 90

    Textured Materials 91

    Creating a Tactile Garden 92

Chapter 26. Hearing 93

    The Journey of Sound: From Ear to Brain 93

    The Emotional Landscape of Hearing 93

    The Primal Sounds of Nature 94

    Cultivating a Deeper Connection with Hearing 94

    Conclusion 95

Chapter 27. Creating a Natural Symphony in the City 96
Natural Sound Features 96
Creating an Urban Natural Symphony 97
Conclusion 98

Chapter 28. Sight 99
The Journey of Light: From Eye to Brain 99
The Emotional Landscape of Sight 100
Visual Strain in Urban Environments 100
Cultivating a Deeper Connection with Sight 101
Conclusion 101

Chapter 29. Urban Spaces with Natural Views 102
Creating a Natural Viewing Experience in the City 102
Creating an Illusion of Expanse 103
Conclusion 104

Chapter 30. Taste 105
The Journey of Taste: From Mouth to Brain 105
The Five Primary Tastes 105
The Role of Smell in Enhancing Taste 106
The Challenge of Artificiality in Modern Food 106
The Impact on Our Taste Experience 107
Reconnecting with Natural Flavors 107
Conclusion 108

Chapter 31. Rediscovering Authentic Flavors 109
Creating a Natural Taste Oasis in the City 111
Conclusion 111

Epilogue: Rediscovering Emotion 112
The State of Overwhelm 112
Nature's Call to Reconnect 112
Embracing the Moment 113
Conclusion 113

A Song of Healing 114
Appendix: The Countryside Code 118
   Respect Other People 118
   Protect the Natural Environment 118
   Enjoy the Outdoors Responsibly 118
   Keep Dogs Under Control 119
   Follow Signs and Advice 119
   Conclusion 119

Introduction

Welcome to **Healing Through Nature: Mindful Practices for Emotional Healing**.

This book describes a journey to help you feel whole and balanced again by connecting with the natural world around you.

Always Busy

In our busy modern world we can often feel that we are pulled in all different directions by social expectations, professional demands and self-expectations.

- **Social Expectations:** In our personal lives we try to live up to what other people expect of us.
- **Professional Demands:** At work we try to be a perfect employee and flawless professional.
- **Self-Expectations:** Sometimes we expect ourselves to be the perfect all-rounder, pleasing everyone we know the utmost.

This constant exertion can leave us feeling conflicted, ineffective, and emotionally off-balance. Additionally, we may feel too busy to pay attention to the relationships that are truly the most important in our lives.

Nature as a Guide

Multiple studies have shown that spending time in nature reduces stress, improves our mood, and enhances cognitive function.

1. **Stress Reduction**: Research from Cornell University found that spending just 10 minutes in a natural setting can significantly reduce both physical and mental stress, making individuals feel happier and more relaxed (https://news.cornell.edu/stories/2020/02/spending-time-nature-reduces-stress-research-finds).
2. **Mood Improvement**: Studies reviewed by the American Psychological Association indicate that exposure to nature can lead to improved mood and reduced risk of psychiatric disorders. This is due to the calming and restorative effects that natural environments have on the mind (https://e360.yale.edu/features/ecopsychology-how-immersion-

in-nature-benefits-your-health).

3. **Cognitive Enhancement**: The concept of "Attention Restoration Theory," developed by Rachel and Stephen Kaplan, suggests that nature allows for a type of effortless attention that helps the brain recover from the fatigue caused by sustained focus on demanding tasks. This can lead to improved cognitive functions such as better focus and working memory (ibid.).

Overall, these findings suggest that integrating time in nature into our daily routines can provide significant emotional health benefits and improve our overall well-being.

Conclusion

In the busy modern world, we tend to lose bits of ourselves along the way, and we sometimes need to go looking for those missing pieces. Reconnecting with nature can provide a gentle, supportive path to re-finding wholeness.

By immersing yourself in the natural world, you can create space for stillness and self-awareness. The exercises and mindful practices in this book are designed to help you tap into this natural wisdom, guiding you toward a harmonious and fulfilling life.

Embrace this journey with an open heart and mind, and allow nature to support you in rediscovering your authentic self. Each step you take in nature is a step toward greater peace, balance, and well-being.

Morning mist, by the author

Section I: The Problem with Modernity

New York City, Wikimedia Commons

Chapter 1. The Industrial Revolution

The Industrial Revolution, starting in the late 18th century, drastically transformed human society. It moved us from agrarian lifestyles deeply connected to nature, to urban, industrialized environments filled with machines and artificiality. While this brought technological and economic progress, it also profoundly changed how we live and relate to the natural world.

Before factories, human life was intertwined with nature. Daily activities followed the sun's cycle, and the land was more than a source of sustenance; it was central to identity and community. Villages thrived among forests, rivers, and fields, drawing resources in moderation to ensure survival and well-being.

Pieter Bruegel the Elder- The Harvesters, Wikimedia Commons

As industries grew, people migrated to cities for factory jobs, severing these natural connections. The rhythmic pace of nature gave way to the relentless schedules of industrial work. The symphony of birds and rustling leaves was replaced by the noise of machinery and bustling streets.

In this urbanized world, humanity created a landscape of concrete, steel, and glass, governed by artificial light and man-made time. This "advanced" environment distanced us from the natural patterns that ground our existence.

James Nasmyth's steam hammer, 1900. E Zimmer

Disconnected from nature, people faced new health challenges.

- Factories and urban homes, lacked natural light and fresh air and led to declines in overall health.

- Noise, pollution and stress increased anxiety and nervousness.

- The shift from natural living eroded community bonds, replacing them with isolated, individualistic lifestyles.

The deep connection to the land, a source of identity and continuity, was lost, leaving a void in modern urban life.

Satellite view of New York City, Google Earth

Today, there is a growing recognition of the need to reconnect with nature:

- Environmental challenges like climate change and biodiversity loss highlight the urgency of restoring our relationship with the natural world.

- The benefits of nature for mental and physical health prompt a re-evaluation of our city-bound lifestyles.

To address these challenges, we must re-enter the world of nature, seeking out a natural mindset that recreates our connection to the environment and our natural selves.

By rediscovering and reintegrating natural living patterns, we can restore balance and harmony in our lives. This journey isn't about returning to the past but forging a new relationship with nature that respects and honours our modern realities. It's about finding sustainable, healthy ways to coexist with the natural world.

Rediscovering the natural connection can bring a sense of place, purpose, and well-being that transcends the confines of our industrialized world.

Walking in the Lake District, Wikimedia Commons

Chapter 2. Beyond Luxury Retreats

The idea of escaping to a luxury countryside resort is very tempting. These retreats promise a combination of serene landscapes, peaceful environments together with luxurious accommodations, and seem like the perfect way to unwind from urban stress.

Nevertheless these five-star resorts fall short of fostering a true, restorative connection to nature.

Taujėnai Manor, Wikipedia Commons

Luxury resorts offer maximum comfort and convenience, they cater to every need and desire, from gourmet meals to spa treatments. However, it is exactly these enjoyable experiences that create an artificial bubble that isolates guests from the raw, unfiltered experience of nature.

Instead of interacting with nature directly, guests engage with a sanitized version that lacks the authenticity and unpredictability of true, natural settings.

The Importance of Immersion

To truly benefit from nature, we must engage with it directly and intimately. This means leaving the comfort of luxury resorts and immersing ourselves in natural environments without modern buffers.

Hiking across uneven terrain, feeling the wind on our faces, and listening to the unfiltered sounds of immediate wildlife are experiences that can't be replicated by a five-star retreat.

Connecting with nature requires authentic experiences that engage all the senses and challenge both body and mind. Five star resorts guarantee we will be saved from discomfort, but it is exactly the breaking away from urban comforts that plays a crucial role in deepening our connection to nature.

Facing natural elements—whether it's a sudden rainstorm, a steep mountain trail, or the chill of a morning breeze—reminds us of our place within the natural world. These moments of discomfort challenge us, ground us, and ultimately lead to a greater sense of accomplishment and connection.

Conclusion

While luxury resorts offer many pleasures, they are unlikely to provide a deep, restorative connection to nature. To truly benefit from nature's healing powers, we must embrace authentic, immersive experiences beyond the confines of luxury and comfort.

By stepping into the wild, facing natural challenges, and engaging directly with nature, we can rediscover the profound peace and balance that nature offers, reconnecting with the rhythms and patterns that have sustained humanity for millennia.

Camping in Sierra Nevada National Park, Wikimedia Commons

Chapter 3. The Machine

Before the Industrial Revolution, people lived closely with nature. Life depended on the land, and daily activities were deeply connected to the natural world. The rhythms of life were guided by the rising and setting of the sun, the changing seasons, and the cycles of planting and harvest.

In those times, people had a strong bond with nature. For example:

- **Tilling the Soil:** Farmers worked the land with their hands and simple tools, understanding the needs of the soil and the seasons.
- **Harvesting Crops:** Harvest time was a community effort, bringing families and neighbours together to gather the fruits of their labour. This created a sense of gratitude and respect for the earth.
- **Baking Bread:** Turning harvested grains into bread was a hands-on process, reminding people of the hard work and the natural gifts needed to produce food.

Every day was a balance of hard work and respect for nature, fostering a deep connection to the land and the people who worked it.

Man Ploughing with a White Horse, Munch Museum

The Rise of the Machine

The Industrial Revolution changed everything. It brought machines and factories, transforming how we lived and worked. People moved from farms to cities, and machines took over tasks that were once done by hand.

Today, our lives are filled with machines. We rely on cars to get us places, traffic lights to guide us, computers and smartphones for communication, and airplanes to travel long distances. Even the roads we drive on and the buildings we live in are made by machines.

Machines have brought many benefits, but they also have their drawbacks. At their core, machines are non-human entities, therefore the more we associate with and identify with machines, the further we move away from our own inner humanity.

Some specific issues that the widespread use of machines has led to are:

- **Environmental Impact:** Industrial farming often prioritizes short-term gains over long-term sustainability, leading to soil depletion, loss of biodiversity, and pollution.
- **Loss of Traditional Skills:** The knowledge and practices of traditional farming have faded as industrial methods took over.
- **Disconnection from Food Sources:** Many people no longer understand where their food comes from, losing appreciation for the natural world and its resources.

When we rely too heavily on machines, we risk losing touch with what makes us human - our creativity, our connection to nature, and our ability to care.

Mindful Practices for Reconnecting

Mindful activities can deepen our connection to nature and restore a sense of balance. Here are some exercises to help you reconnect:

Harvest Reflection

- **Location:** Find a quiet spot in a garden, park, or backyard.
- **Preparation:** Choose a piece of fresh produce like an apple or carrot.
- **Activity:** Sit quietly, hold the produce, and reflect on its journey from seed to harvest. Imagine the sunlight, rain, soil, and human effort that contributed to its growth.

  Spend 10-15 minutes fostering a sense of connection and gratitude for what the earth provides us.

Animal Connection

- **Location:** Visit a local farm, petting zoo, or animal sanctuary.
- **Activity:** Sit quietly near the animals, focusing on the sounds, smells, and sights around you. Observe their behaviours and reflect on the relationship between humans and animals.

  Spend 10-15 minutes fostering a sense of connection and gratitude for what animals provide us.

Planting Seeds

- **Location:** Find a garden or natural area where you can plant seeds.
- **Activity:** Prepare the soil, hold the seeds in your hand, and focus on their potential. As you plant each seed, reflect on the cycle of growth and the nurturing power of nature.

  Spend 10-15 minutes feeling the power of renewal of the natural growth cycle.

Conclusion

The rise of machines has significantly changed our world, making life more convenient but also distancing us from our natural roots and our own humanity. As we become more reliant on machines, we risk losing the personal, caring way we once interacted with the world around us.

Reconnecting with a natural, machine-free existence helps us rediscover these essential aspects of our humanity. Through mindful practices and traditional activities, we can restore our bond with nature and nurture our ability to care for the world and each other.

This approach not only fosters a healthier relationship with the earth but also brings balance, gratitude, and sustainability into our lives.

Harvesters, Anna Ancher

Section II. Natural Being

As natural beings in an artificial city environment, we often find ourselves adopting artificial patterns of behaviour that are at odds to our true selves.

This section explores artificial patterns of behaviour that we may take for granted as being a normal part of everyday life, but which can lead us away from a true connection to our selves and others.

Wheat, by the author

Chapter 4. Hyperthinking

In today's world, we're encouraged to think constantly. Whether we're planning our day, worrying about catching the bus, or stressing over work details, our brains are always active.

Thinking Too Much

While it's good to think things through, too much thinking can actually be harmful. Here's why:

- **Overthinking Everything:** When we overthink, we analyse every little detail of every situation. Instead of making decisions and moving forward, we get stuck in a cycle of "what ifs" and "maybes." For example, imagine you have to give a presentation at work. Instead of preparing and then relaxing, you might spend hours worrying about every possible thing that could go wrong. This not only wastes time but also increases your stress levels.

- **Preventing Us from Being Present:** The constant flow of thoughts can keep us from enjoying the present moment. Think about the last time you were with friends or family. Were you fully engaged, or were you thinking about work, your to-do list, or other worries? When our minds are always racing, we miss out on the simple joys of life, like a beautiful sunset, a good conversation, or a delicious meal.

- **Stress and Anxiety:** Overthinking often leads to stress and anxiety. When we constantly worry about what might happen, our bodies respond as if we're in danger. This can cause physical symptoms like headaches, muscle tension, and trouble sleeping. For instance, if you're always thinking about potential problems at work, your body stays in a state of high alert, making it hard to relax and enjoy life.

By thinking too much, we can lose mental clarity and the ability to think usefully, positively and constructively.

Robust Thinking

Robust thinking refers to the ability to think clearly, critically, and effectively, even under pressure. It involves maintaining clarity, flexibility, and adaptability.

- **Mental Clarity:** Robust thinking helps us maintain clarity of thought, making it easier to solve problems and make decisions efficiently.

- **Stress Reduction:** By thinking robustly, we can reduce unnecessary stress and anxiety. Instead of worrying about things, we can handle life's challenges calmly and rationally.

- **Improved Productivity:** When we think robustly, we can make effective decisions. This leads to better results and a sense of accomplishment.

Instead of getting caught up in overthinking, robust thinking allows us to make decisions confidently and handle challenges without becoming overwhelmed.

Mindfulness Exercises for Robust Thinking

Nature offers a sanctuary from the relentless pace of modern life. Immersing ourselves in natural environments helps quiet the mind, allowing us to break free from hyperthinking. The simple act of being in nature can restore a sense of balance and perspective, offering a mental reset.

Here are some mindfulness exercises to practice in nature, designed to help escape hyperthinking and achieve robust thinking instead:

Sky Gazing Reflection

1. Think of an issue you want to clarify and resolve.
2. Find a comfortable spot to lie down in an open area.
3. Look up at the sky, watching the clouds drift by.
4. Allow your thoughts to float away with the clouds, observing without attachment or judgment.
5. Spend 10-15 minutes simply being present with the sky.
6. Turn your mind back to the issue you wanted to think about.

7. Let your thoughts form naturally around the subject and trust your intuition.

Thinking Walk

1. Think of an issue you want to clarify and resolve.

2. Walk through a natural setting (if possible, outside of the city); pay attention to the feel of the earth beneath your feet, the sounds around you, and the air on your skin.

3. Only allow yourself to ponder the issue you want to think about as a background, secondary thinking to your main focus on the natural things around you.

4. Continue walking till the issue has resolved itself through your natural settings.

Structured Reflection

Regularly take time to reflect on your thoughts and experiences. Structured reflection helps you analyse your thinking patterns and make adjustments as needed.

Here's how you can practice structured reflection:

- **Journaling:** Set aside a fixed time each day (between 10 minutes to half an hour, as needed) to write about your daily experiences and thoughts. This practice can help you process your emotions and gain insights into your thinking patterns.

- **Goal Setting:** Reflect on your goals and the steps you're taking to achieve them. Adjust your plans as needed to stay on track without overburdening yourself.

Conclusion

In our hyperanalytical society, escaping hyperthinking is essential for mental well-being.

Through mindful engagement with the natural world, we can rediscover the peace and balance that are often lost in the hustle and bustle of modern life. Embrace the tranquillity of nature, and let it guide you to a clearer, calmer state of mind and to better, healthier decisions.

Chapter 5. Complexity

In the past, the daily life of a villager was relatively straightforward. Survival was the main focus—food, shelter, and community. Today, our lives are filled with work responsibilities, family obligations, social media interactions, and a constant influx of information.

If the villager of old had ten things to consider and twenty possible destinations, we have hundreds of concerns and thousands of places to be.

The Maze of Life

This increase in complexity often makes our lives feel like navigating a vast and confusing maze. We are confronted with a myriad of choices in planning our path through life, from selecting a career and choosing where to live, to deciding how to spend our leisure time. Advertising bombards us with countless options for products and services, each promising to improve our lives. Additionally, the sheer number of opportunities available—from educational programs to travel destinations—can be both exhilarating and overwhelming.

Our brains are not designed to handle this level of complexity. Our cognitive capacities are limited, and when we exceed these limits, we experience stress and cognitive overload. This can lead to feelings of anxiety and a sense of being lost in a never-ending maze.

Auckland Spaghetti Junction, Wikimedia Commons

Clarity through Nature

When we achieve a natural state of mind through mindfulness, we align ourselves with the inherent rhythms and wisdom of the natural world. This connection allows us to tap into our intuition and inner clarity, enabling us to make decisions that are naturally correct for us.

In this natural state of mind, we become more attuned to our true needs and desires, free from external pressures and distractions. We can channel the life force of nature, which brings a sense of calm and balance. This heightened awareness helps us to see our options more clearly and to discern the path that best aligns with our authentic self. By being present and connected to the moment, we trust our instincts and inner guidance, leading to choices that feel inherently right and fulfilling.

For example, instead of feeling overwhelmed by the myriad of career options and advice from others, a person in a natural state of mind can sense which path resonates with their core values and passions. Similarly, when faced with personal or professional dilemmas, this state of mind provides the clarity to choose what truly feels right, rather than what seems expected or conventional.

Through mindfulness and meditation, we cultivate this natural state of mind, which acts as a compass guiding us through the complexities of life with greater ease and confidence.

The Thinker, By Edvard Munch

Musée Rodin, Public Domain

Mindfulness Exercises for Navigating Complexity

To help you navigate the complexities of modern life, here are some mindfulness exercises designed to let you naturally determine your own path by channelling the life force of nature and enabling you to come to the naturally correct decision given various life choices.

Grounding Meditation

- Find a quiet natural setting such as a forest, park, or beach.
- Sit or lie down on the ground and close your eyes. Take slow, deep breaths, and focus on the sensation of the earth beneath you. Allow any stress or tension to flow out of you and into the earth.
- Spend 10-15 minutes in this meditation, feeling grounded and connected to nature.
- Once you achieve a state of natural calmness, think through the decision you need to make.

Water Flow Meditation

- Sit by a flowing stream or river.
- Close your eyes and focus on the sound of the water flowing. Imagine your thoughts and decisions as leaves floating on the water, being carried away by the current.
- Allow the natural flow of the water to help you release any overwhelming thoughts or emotions. Spend 10-15 minutes in this meditation, feeling the calming effects of the water.
- Once you achieve a state of natural calmness, think through the decision you need to make.

Nature Walk Reflection

- Walk through a natural setting such as a forest, park, or beach.
- Focus on the feel of the earth beneath your feet, the sounds around you, and the air on your skin. As you walk, allow your thoughts to come and go naturally.
- Consider any decisions you need to make, but keep your main focus on the natural surroundings. Continue walking until you feel a sense of clarity and resolution.

Conclusion

Navigating the maze of modern life is undoubtedly challenging, but through mindfulness exercises and a deeper connection with nature, we can channel the life force of nature to help us determine our own path and make naturally correct decisions. Embrace these practices to navigate the complexities of life with greater ease and confidence.

In this way we can create a more balanced and fulfilling life amidst the complexity of the modern world.

Istanbul, Iam Hogir

Chapter 6: Distraction

In the bustling city, where skyscrapers stretch towards the sky and artificial lighting blurs the divide between day and night, we often find ourselves swept up in a relentless tide of activity. In this artificial world, distractions come in many forms, from the incessant ping of notifications on our devices to the lure of binge-watching television shows.

These distractions offer a temporary escape from the stresses of daily life but ultimately pull us further away from introspection and self-awareness. They create a barrier between our true selves and the world around us, making it harder to connect with our inner thoughts and emotions.

This is because as long as we are distracted, we are distracted from ourselves. Distractions prevent us from looking inward and understanding our true thoughts, feelings, and desires. When we are constantly occupied by external stimuli, we have little time or mental space to reflect on our own lives and experiences.

Without time for introspection, we drift aimlessly, feeling increasingly disconnected from our inner selves.

Piccadilly Circus, Wikimedia Commons

Self-Possession

Self-possession is the opposite of distraction. Self-possession allows us to remain centred and composed, regardless of external circumstances; this allows us to navigate the complexities of life with calm and purpose.

- Embracing self-possession allows us to live authentically. We no longer feel the need to conform to external expectations or hide behind facades. Instead, we can express our true selves and connect with others on a deeper, more genuine level.

- Self-possession empowers us to take control of our lives. We become proactive rather than reactive, making conscious choices that reflect our true desires and aspirations. This empowerment leads to greater satisfaction and a sense of accomplishment.

- Self-possession allows us to discern what truly matters to us and make decisions that align with our values. This helps us stay focused on our goals and aspirations, guiding us towards a more fulfilling life.

Through self-possession, we acquire the remarkable ability to not become overawed by our surroundings, however grandiose and impressive they may be.

In a world that seeks to overwhelm and grab our attention, self-possession grants us the strength to remain steadfast and grounded. Whether we stand before the towering skyscrapers of a bustling metropolis or in the presence of influential figures, self-possession allows us to maintain our sense of self and purpose.

Mindfulness Exercises

One powerful way to cultivate self-possession is by immersing ourselves in nature. The natural world offers a sanctuary from the constant demands of modern life, providing a tranquil environment where we can reflect and find clarity.

Finding Clarity in Stillness

Nature's inherent stillness can help quiet the city noise that reverberates in our minds. By immersing ourselves in natural environments, we can find the self-awareness and the self-possession that allow us to see beyond the immediate demands of daily life.

- Find a quiet spot by a stream or river.
- Sit comfortably and close your eyes. Focus on the sounds of the water flowing, birds singing, and leaves rustling. Let go of any intrusive thoughts, allowing the natural sounds to fill your mind. Embrace the sense of calm that comes from this focused listening, using it to clear your mind and gain perspective on your life.
- As you feel the tranquillity settling in, reflect on your current state of self-awareness and any areas of your life where you feel overwhelmed and disconnected.

This exercise helps you centre your mind, fostering self-possession by quieting external distractions and deepening your inner focus.

Visualizing Your Future Self

While connecting with nature, you can also use this opportunity to visualize yourself as you will be in five years if you continue on your current trajectory. This exercise can provide profound insights into whether you are living a life aligned with your true desires and values, or whether you are being swept along in the city noise.

- Find a serene natural setting where you feel at peace.
- Sit down comfortably, close your eyes, and take a few deep breaths to centre yourself. Imagine yourself five years into the future. See yourself living according to your current path and choices.
- Observe your surroundings, your lifestyle, and your emotional state.
- Pay attention to how this future vision makes you feel. Are you happy, fulfilled, and content? Or do you feel trapped, stressed, and unfulfilled? Ask yourself, "Is this really what I want from life?"
- If the answer is no, ponder why you are continuing on this path. What invisible threads or external expectations are influencing your choices?

If possible, bring a journal and write down your reflections and insights.

Use this information to guide you in making changes that align more closely with your true self. This exercise promotes self-possession by clarifying your values and empowering you to make decisions that reflect your authentic desires.

Conclusion

The never-ending distractions of modern life can prevent us from truly connecting with ourselves. By seeking peace and connection in nature, we can find our way back to our true selves.

Through mindful practices and a deeper connection with the natural world, we can break free from the distractions that keep us from introspection and self-awareness. Embrace these practices to cultivate self-possession, and so enabling yourself to navigate the complexities of life with calm, purpose, and authenticity.

A Stream, Darya Grey Owl

Chapter 7: Professionalism

In our professional lives, there is often immense pressure to project an image of success and competence.

The modern workplace, with its rigid expectations and relentless drive for productivity, can lead us into a cycle of maintaining a facade of perfection which impacts our well-being and draws us away from authenticity.

Off to the Office, by David Kouakou

The Weight of Expectations

Corporations demand perfection and predictability, therefore from the moment we step into the workplace, we are conditioned to maintain a constant appearance of flawlessness. We wear the mask of professionalism our entire professional lives, hiding our true emotions and desires behind a veneer of competence and success.

This facade demands that we are always "on," always striving to meet unrealistic standards and suppressing our vulnerabilities.

The pressure to conform begins subtly. There is the unspoken expectation to dress a certain way, speak a certain way, and behave a certain way. The office becomes a stage, and we become actors in a play, each role meticulously crafted to project the image of the perfect professional.

The Pressure of the Facade

The constant effort to maintain this facade can be mentally and emotionally exhausting. When we are perpetually focused on appearing perfect, we lose touch with our true selves and our genuine aspirations.

Upholding this facade can lead to stress and anxiety. We become trapped in a cycle of self-imposed expectations, fearing that any display of imperfection will be judged harshly by our peers and superiors.

This relentless pursuit of an unattainable ideal can erode our self-esteem and lead to burnout. We fear that a single crack in the facade will expose us to scrutiny and judgment, so we plaster on another layer of false confidence, further distancing ourselves from our authentic selves.

Strength of Character

Contrary to the superficial confidence projected by the facade of professionalism, real strength of character lies in authenticity and self-possession. This involves an inner strength that is not dependent on external validation but is grounded in a deep understanding and acceptance of oneself.

Real strength of character means you have the confidence to walk into the office and be yourself, engage in real non-ritualistic behaviour and express your concerns in an authentic and engaging way.

This authenticity fosters genuine connections with others. When we are honest about our strengths and weaknesses, we invite others to do the same, creating an environment of trust and collaboration. This can lead to more meaningful professional relationships and a more supportive workplace culture.

Authenticity gives us:

1. **Enhanced Resilience:** By accepting our imperfections, we are better equipped to handle failures and setbacks, viewing them as opportunities for growth rather than threats to our artificial self-worth.

2. **Improved Well-Being:** Maintaining a facade is exhausting and can lead to burnout. In contrast, authenticity promotes physical and emotional well-being.

3. **Stronger Leadership:** Authentic leaders inspire trust and loyalty. Their genuine approach fosters a positive organizational culture and encourages others to bring their true selves to work.

4. **Creative Problem-Solving:** When people are not constrained by the need to appear perfect, they are more open to exploring new ideas and taking risks.

Certainly walking into an office and being professional is a challenge, but this is a challenge that we can rise up to, by responding from our true authentic selves, rather than a challenge that we must be swamped by, by assuming a plastic workplace façade.

Reimagining Ourselves Through Mindfulness

The challenge of maintaining professionalism while being true to ourselves can be addressed through nature-based mindfulness reflections.

Engaging with nature during work hours and while in work clothes is particularly beneficial, as this allows us to integrate mindfulness into our professional routine, bridging the gap between our professional and authentic, natural selves.

Mindful Walks During Work Breaks

One of the simplest yet most effective nature-based mindfulness practices is a mindful walk during work breaks.

- Find a quiet park or green space near your office.
- As you walk, focus on the sensations of your feet touching the ground, the sound of leaves rustling in the wind, and the scent of the grass and the earth.
- Fantasize that you have entered an entirely new natural world in which your office does not exist.

Being in your work clothes will allow you to integrate this state of mindfulness into your professional identity, helping you maintain a sense of calm and authenticity throughout your workday.

Nature Meditation During Lunch Breaks

Find a peaceful spot in nature close to your workplace where you can sit comfortably.

- Close your eyes and take a few deep breaths, cantering yourself.
- Begin to focus on the sounds around you—the chirping of birds, the rustling of leaves, the flowing of water.
- Allow these natural sounds to guide you into a state of deep relaxation and mindfulness.
- Visualize yourself shedding your professional facade, layer by layer, until only your true self remains.

This practice, conducted during your lunch break and in your work clothes, ensures that you return to work with a refreshed and authentic mindset.

Observing Wildlife

Observing animals in their natural habitat can provide powerful insights into authenticity. This does not only apply to impressive animals in a farm, zoo or safari; it also applies to the most ordinary wildlife that we can see in a nearby park or at home.

- Spend time watching birds, insects, or other wildlife in a nearby park, and notice how they live authentically in the present moment.
- Let this observation inspire you to embrace your own authentic nature.

Doing this in your work clothes and during work hours helps you carry this inspiration back into the office.

Conclusion

Walking into an office and still being ourselves is indeed a challenge, but it is one that we can rise to by responding from our natural selves rather than by assuming a plastic workplace facade.

By regularly engaging in nature-based mindfulness practices during work hours and in work clothes, we can cultivate a sense of authenticity that carries over into our professional lives.

Chapter 8. Information Overload

In today's digital age, we are constantly bombarded with an overwhelming amount of information. From the news we read to the movies we watch, our brains are continuously processing vast quantities of data.

This relentless flow of information can lead to a loss of clarity, mental fatigue, and a sense of being overwhelmed.

Understanding Information Overload

Information overload occurs when we are exposed to more information than our brains can effectively process. This can happen through various channels:

- **Digital Media:** Constant updates from social media, news websites, and other online platforms.
- **Entertainment:** The sensory overload from movies, television shows, and video games.
- **Work and Daily Life:** The continuous stream of emails, messages, and notifications.

The human brain is designed to process information, but it has limits. When we exceed these limits, we can experience mental fatigue, stress and anxiety, decreased focus and impaired decision-making.

The Brain's Processing Power

To understand the impact of information overload, consider the example of watching a movie. Every second of a film consists of multiple frames, each containing a wealth of visual and auditory data. Our brains must process each frame, interpret the visual cues, understand the dialogue, and follow the storyline. This requires significant cognitive effort, and when compounded by other sources of information, it can quickly lead to overload.

Even after we have finished watching a movie, our brains continue to process the information subconsciously. This means that hours later, our minds are still working through each frame, analysing and integrating the data. This ongoing processing can contribute to mental fatigue and a sense of being overwhelmed, as our brains are constantly working to make sense of the vast amount of information to which they have been exposed.

Nature as an Antidote to Information Overload

Nature provides a refuge from the constant barrage of information. The simplicity and tranquillity of natural environments offer a much-needed break for our overworked minds.

Here's how nature can help:

- **Reduced Stimuli:** Natural settings typically have fewer stimuli compared to urban environments, allowing our brains to rest and recover.
- **Mindfulness:** Nature encourages us to be present and mindful, helping to clear our minds of clutter and distractions.
- **Restorative Effects:** Studies have shown that spending time in nature can reduce stress, improve mood, and enhance cognitive function.

Mindfulness Exercises for Overcoming Information Overload

Here are five mindfulness exercises designed to help you unburden your mind and find clarity through nature:

Forest Breathing

- Find a quiet spot in a forest or wooded area where you can sit comfortably.
- Close your eyes and take slow, deep breaths, focusing on the fresh forest air entering your lungs.
- With each inhale, imagine the clean, crisp air clearing away the mental clutter.
- With each exhale, release any stress or anxiety, letting it dissipate into the forest.
- Spend 10-15 minutes in this meditation, allowing the forest's tranquillity to restore your mind.

Stream Visualization

- Sit by a flowing stream or river, focusing on the sound of the water.
- Close your eyes and visualize your thoughts as leaves floating on the water.
- Imagine the stream carrying away each leaf, one by one, as you let go of the overload of information.

- Reflect on the calm and clarity that comes as the leaves drift away.
- Meditate for 10-15 minutes, using the stream's flow to cleanse your mind.

Sky Gazing
- Lie down in an open field or a quiet spot where you can see the sky.
- Look up at the sky, watching the clouds drift by or the stars twinkle.
- Allow your mind to wander and imagine the vastness of the sky absorbing your worries and information overload.
- Focus on the infinite space and let your thoughts dissolve into the sky.
- Spend 10-15 minutes in this meditation, feeling a sense of expansiveness and mental freedom.

Nature's Sounds
- Find a quiet spot in nature where you can sit comfortably and listen to the sounds around you.
- Close your eyes and focus on the natural sounds—birds singing, leaves rustling, water flowing.
- Allow these sounds to fill your mind, gently pushing out any intrusive thoughts or information overload.
- Reflect on the simplicity and beauty of these natural sounds and let them bring you peace.
- Spend 10-15 minutes in this meditation, allowing nature's sounds to soothe and clear your mind.

Conclusion

In our modern world, information overload is a common challenge that can lead to mental fatigue, stress, and decreased cognitive function. By reconnecting with nature, we can give our minds the break they need, reducing the constant influx of information and allowing for restoration and clarity.

Chapter 9. The Need to Own

In our consumer-driven society, we are often led to believe that joy comes from acquiring more - more possessions, more achievements, more recognition. Advertisements and glitzy store-fronts constantly send us a message that we need to buy more things to feel good.

However, the true joy of living is not found in material wealth but in the richness of experiences, connections, and moments of genuine pleasure.

Oranges and Lemons, Vincent Van Gogh

Joie de Vivre: The Joy of Living

Joie de vivre, or the joy of living, is a French phrase that captures the essence of a carefree enjoyment of life. It's about finding happiness in the simple, everyday moments and appreciating the beauty around us. This concept encourages us to shift our focus away from material possessions and societal expectations, and instead find delight in the present moment.

Nature, with its unending beauty and tranquillity, offers us a perfect backdrop to rediscover and cultivate this joy. When we immerse ourselves in nature, we embrace simplicity. We are reminded that life's greatest joys are often the simplest ones: the sound of birds singing, the feel of the grass under our feet, the sight of a breathtaking sunset.

Nature provides a perfect setting to experience this simplicity, as it strips away the distractions of modern life and allows us to focus on what truly matters.

- **Letting Go of Excess**: Nature encourages us to let go of unnecessary clutter - both physical and mental. Without the trappings of modern life, we can focus on the essentials and find joy in simplicity.
- **Finding Humility**: In the vastness of nature, we are reminded of our small place in the grand scheme of things. This perspective fosters humility and helps us appreciate the simple, yet profound, aspects of life.

Mindfulness Exercises for Embracing Simplicity

Practicing mindfulness in natural settings can help us cultivate a sense of simplicity and fulfilment. Here are five exercises to help you achieve this natural state of being:

Barefoot Grounding Meditation

- Find a quiet, grassy area where you can walk barefoot.
- Slowly walk, paying attention to the sensations of the earth beneath your feet.
- With each step, imagine any stress or unnecessary thoughts being absorbed by the ground.
- Continue this practice for 10-15 minutes, feeling grounded and connected to the earth.

Nature Observation Meditation

- Choose a natural scene to observe, such as a tree, a flowing stream, or a meadow.
- Sit comfortably and focus your gaze on the scene, taking in every detail.
- Notice the colors, shapes, movements, and sounds. Allow your mind to be fully absorbed in the observation.
- Let your thoughts and emotions flow naturally, observing them without judgment. Spend 10-20 minutes in this mindful observation.

Imagining Simplicity Meditation

- Choose a simple path through the countryside and begin walking slowly.
- As you walk, imagine a state where you possess nothing in the world besides the clothes you are wearing. Let go of any thoughts about possessions or achievements.
- Initially, you may experience a sense of panic as the things you think you are dependent on are "taken away." Recognize this feeling without judgment.
- To overcome the panic, focus on your breath. Take slow, deep breaths, inhaling for a count of four, holding for a count of four, exhaling for a count of four, and holding again for a count of four.
- Shift your focus to the present moment and your surroundings—the trees, flowers, sky. Acknowledge that, despite the imagined loss of possessions, you are still whole and present.
- Embrace the sense of freedom and simplicity that comes from having nothing but yourself. Spend 20-30 minutes in this mindful walk, appreciating the simplicity of nature and the essence of your being.

Sun and Shadow Meditation

- Sit or lie down in a place where you can observe the interplay of sunlight and shadows.
- Close your eyes and feel the warmth of the sun and the coolness of the shadows on your skin.
- Reflect on the balance between light and dark, fullness and emptiness.
- Meditate on this balance for 15-20 minutes, embracing the simplicity of natural cycles.

Nature's Gift Meditation
- Find a natural object, such as a stone, leaf, or flower.
- Hold the object in your hand and observe it closely—its texture, color, shape.
- Reflect on the fact that this object exists perfectly as it is, without needing to be anything more.
- Meditate on this for 10-15 minutes, finding contentment in the simplicity of nature's gifts.

Returning to Civilization

After spending time in nature and embracing simplicity, you may find that your perspective on life has shifted. This practice can help you appreciate the abundance that exists in your everyday life, fostering a sense of gratitude and contentment.

- **Appreciating Everyday Comforts**: Returning to civilization, you may notice a newfound appreciation for the comforts and conveniences you previously took for granted.
- **Valuing Relationships**: The simplicity of nature can help you recognize the value of genuine human connections over material possessions or social status.
- **Finding Joy in Small Things**: By reconnecting with the simple pleasures of nature, you can bring this sense of joy and contentment into your daily life, finding happiness in the small things.

Conclusion

By connecting with nature, we can let go of our dependency on material possessions and find contentment in the simplicity of our surroundings.

This practice not only helps us appreciate the natural world but also enhances our gratitude for the abundance in our everyday lives.

Section III: Self

In our fast-paced modern world, it is easy to lose touch with our inner selves. The constant demands of work, social obligations, and the relentless noise of urban living creates a barrier between us and our true nature.

Subsequently, we often find ourselves living identities that have been loaned to us by societal expectations, familial pressures, and professional demands, rather than living our authentic selves.

The section on "Self" in this book is designed to guide you on a journey of rediscovery, helping you reconnect with your true identity through the healing and restorative power of nature.

Footsteps in the Sand, pickpik.com

Chapter 11. Peace of Mind

In our fast-paced modern world, the pursuit of peace of mind is more important than ever. We often find ourselves juggling multiple responsibilities, facing constant digital distractions, and feeling overwhelmed by the demands of daily life. It's no wonder that finding a sense of calm and clarity can seem elusive.

One of the most effective and accessible ways to cultivate peace of mind is by connecting with nature. By immersing ourselves in the natural world, we can tap into its soothing rhythms and restorative qualities, fostering a profound sense of tranquillity and clarity.

Understanding Peace of Mind

Peace of mind is a state of mental and emotional calmness, with no anxiety, stress, or worry. It is a sense of inner tranquillity that allows us to navigate life's challenges with grace and resilience.

Peace of mind is not the absence of problems but is rather the ability to deal with them effectively. It involves being present, having a clear mind, and maintaining emotional balance even in the face of adversity.

Calm, Wikimedia Commons

How We Lose Peace of Mind

In today's world, several factors contribute to the loss of peace of mind:

- **Constant Distractions**: Digital devices, social media, and the 24/7 news cycle bombard us with information, making it difficult to focus and stay present.

- **Overcommitment**: We often stretch ourselves too thin by taking on too many responsibilities, both personally and professionally.

- **Lack of Boundaries**: Failing to set boundaries in our relationships and work life can lead to a sense of being constantly invaded, with no personal time or personal space to recharge and reflect.

Making a Conscious Decision to Regain Peace of Mind

Regaining peace of mind requires a conscious decision to prioritize it in our lives. Here are steps to help you reclaim your mental tranquillity:

- **Recognize the Importance of Peace of Mind**: Understand that peace of mind is crucial for overall well-being. Acknowledge that without it, other aspects of your life, including physical health and relationships, can suffer.

- **Identify Stressors**: Take time to identify specific sources of stress and anxiety in your life. Knowing what disrupts your peace of mind is the first step toward addressing it.

- **Set Boundaries**: Establish clear boundaries to protect your personal inner space. This could mean setting limits on work hours, reducing screen time, or saying no to additional commitments.

- **Practice Mindfulness**: Incorporate mindfulness practices into your daily routine. Mindfulness helps you stay present and reduces the impact of chaotic thought patterns.

- **Connect with Nature**: Nature has a unique ability to restore peace of mind. Regularly spending time in natural settings can help you disconnect from the chaos and reconnect with your inner calm.

Practical Steps to Find Peace in Nature

Finding peace of mind through nature doesn't require a major lifestyle overhaul. Here are some practical steps you can take to incorporate the calming influence of nature into your daily routine.

- **Make Time for Daily Nature Breaks**: Incorporate short breaks into your day to step outside and connect with nature. Even a few minutes spent walking in a green space or sitting in your backyard can make a difference. Use these moments to observe your surroundings and to let go of lingering stress.

- **Practice Mindful Walking:** Mindful walking involves paying close attention to your surroundings and your natural perceptions as you walk. Choose a setting such as a park or a nature trail, and focus on the sights, sounds, and smells around you. Notice the feeling of the ground beneath your feet and the rhythm of your breath. This can help you stay present and cultivate a sense of peace.

- **Create a Personal Nature Sanctuary**: If regular outings to natural settings aren't feasible, consider creating a small sanctuary at home. Fill your living space with plants, natural materials such as a branch from a forest or a few small rocks, and images of nature. Designate a quiet corner for relaxation and reflection, where you can escape the demands of daily life and reconnect with yourself.

Mindfulness Exercises in Nature

In addition to incorporating nature into your routine, practicing mindfulness in natural settings can significantly enhance your sense of inner peace and well-being.

Here are a few mindfulness exercises to try.

Forest Breathing

- Find a quiet spot in a forest or wooded area.
- Stand or sit comfortably, close your eyes, and take slow, deep breaths.
- Focus on the fresh forest air entering your lungs and the calming effect it has on your body.

Spend 10-15 minutes in this practice, allowing the tranquillity of the forest to wash over you.

Sky Gazing
- Lie down in an open field or a quiet spot where you can see the sky.
- Look up and watch the clouds drift by or the stars twinkle.
- Allow your mind to wander and imagine the vastness of the sky absorbing your worries and information overload.

Spend 10-15 minutes in this meditation, feeling a sense of expansiveness and mental freedom.

Water Reflection
- Sit by a body of water, such as a lake, river, or pond.
- Focus on the reflections in the water and the gentle movement of the surface.
- Close your eyes and visualize the water washing away your stress and worries, leaving you with a sense of peace and clarity.

Spend 10-15 minutes in this practice, feeling the cleansing and healing effects of the water.

Nature Sound Reflection
- Find a quiet spot in nature where you can sit comfortably and listen to the sounds around you.
- Close your eyes and focus on the natural sounds—birds singing, leaves rustling, water flowing.
- Allow these sounds to fill your mind, gently pushing out any intrusive thoughts or worries.
- Reflect on the simplicity of these natural sounds and let them bring you peace.

Spend 10-15 minutes in this meditation.

Conclusion

Peace of mind is not a passive state but a conscious choice. By understanding how we lose it and taking deliberate steps to regain it, we can cultivate a life of calm and clarity.

Incorporating nature into your daily routine and practicing mindfulness in natural settings can significantly enhance your peace of mind. By taking the time to connect with the natural world, you allow yourself to step away from the chaos of modern life and find a sense of calm and clarity.

Chapter 12. Solitude

We are often taught that it is important to be part of the crowd, and to be part of "what's happening". However, it is equally important for us to be able to exist on our own and by ourselves, in order to find the ability to communicate with ourselves, as well as with others.

Nature offers a sanctuary where we can achieve this inner self-communication. In the solitude of nature, we can:

- **Reconnect with Ourselves:** Solitude provides a chance to reconnect with our inner selves and understand our true desires and needs.
- **Gain Clarity:** Without the noise and distractions of the urban world, we can think more clearly and make better decisions.
- **Create a Reference Point**: In the solitude of nature we can reach a calm state of mind which we can always refer back to when we are in the middle of the hustle and bustle of the city.

How to Practice Solitude in Nature

1. **Choose a Location:** Find a place that resonates with you—whether it's a forest, a beach, a mountain, or a park. The key is to choose a location where you feel safe and comfortable.

2. **Set an Intention:** Before you begin, set a clear intention for your time in nature. This could be to find peace, gain clarity, connect with your inner self, or simply to relax.

3. **Disconnect from Technology:** Leave your phone and other digital devices behind or turn them off. This will help you fully immerse yourself in the natural surroundings without distractions.

4. **Be Present:** Focus on being present in the moment. Pay attention to the details around you—the rustling of leaves, the chirping of birds, the feel of the breeze on your skin. Use all your senses to experience the environment fully.

5. **Reflect and Meditate:** Spend time reflecting on your thoughts and feelings. You can meditate, pray, or simply sit quietly. Allow your mind to wander naturally and notice any insights or feelings that arise.

6. **Journal Your Experience:** Bring a journal to record your thoughts and experiences. Writing can help you process your reflections and

solidify any insights gained during your time alone.

7. **Regular Practice:** Make solitude in nature a regular practice. Whether it's once a week or once a month, consistent time spent in nature can have lasting positive effects on your well-being.

Conclusion

Nature offers a sanctuary where we can escape the rushing crowd and find moments of true solitude. By seeking out these quiet, natural spaces, we can reconnect with ourselves, reduce stress, and gain clarity.

Let nature be your refuge, a place where you can find tranquillity and reconnect with your inner self.

Solitude, Vitana Monkam

Chapter 13. Words

Words are incredibly useful, and it would be challenging to navigate our daily lives without them. They allow us to communicate, express emotions, and share ideas. However, too many words can distract us from our inner selves and lead to mental clutter.

The Wordless Inner Self

Our true inner essence is wordless. While we use words to express our feelings, there are moments when language falls short. Common expressions like "I feel it in my heart" or "I can't explain it, but this is how I feel" highlight that, at our core, we rely on feelings and perceptions rather than words. This deep inner self, often referred to as the "heart," exists beyond the confines of language.

When we speak less, our words are more likely to reflect our true inner state. On the other hand, a rush of words can signify a jumble of thoughts disconnected from our genuine feelings. This is why sometimes it's better to say too little rather than too much.

Words and the Modern World

In the modern world, we are bombarded with words. Emails, social media, videos, advertisements, radio, newspapers and TV constantly scream at us. This word-centric environment can pull us into a word-centric existence, making us lose touch with the original, natural source of our words—our wordless inner self.

When we become overly reliant on words, they cease to convey the truth of our inner feelings. Instead, they become a distraction from what we are really feeling inside.

Newspaper rack, pickpik.com

The Wordlessness of Nature

Nature itself is wordless. It communicates through the rustling of leaves, the flow of rivers, and the calls of birds—all without words. This natural wordlessness helps us quiet our minds and tune into the essence of our being. By immersing ourselves in the wordlessness of nature, we create the space to rediscover and connect with our own wordless inner selves.

Mindfulness Exercises for Wordlessness

Here are five mindfulness exercises designed to help you reconnect with your inner wordlessness and natural self:

Silent Nature Walk

- Find a quiet, natural setting for a walk.
- As you walk, focus on the sounds of nature around you—the wind in the trees, the chirping of birds, the rustle of leaves underfoot.
- Avoid speaking and allow your mind to absorb the natural sounds.
- Spend 15-20 minutes walking in silence, tuning into the wordless communication of nature.

Listening Meditation

- Sit comfortably in a natural environment, close your eyes, and focus on the sounds around you.
- Pay attention to each sound without labelling it or thinking about it—just listen.
- Let the natural sounds wash over you, helping you enter a state of inner silence.
- Practice this for 10-15 minutes, allowing yourself to become fully immersed in the wordlessness of nature.

Sky Gazing

- Find a quiet spot where you can lie down and look up at the sky.
- Observe the clouds drifting by or the stars twinkling without trying to describe or analyse what you see.
- Allow your mind to quiet as you focus on the vastness of the sky.
- Spend 10-15 minutes simply gazing and letting go of words.

Water Reflection

- Sit by a body of water, such as a lake, river, or pond.
- Watch the reflections in the water and the movement of its surface.
- Close your eyes and visualize the water washing away your thoughts and words, leaving you with a sense of inner peace.
- Spend 10-15 minutes in this reflective practice, embracing the wordless quality of water.

Forest Breathing

- Find a quiet spot in a forest or wooded area.
- Stand or sit comfortably, close your eyes, and take slow, deep breaths.
- Focus on the fresh forest air entering your lungs and the calming effect it has on your body.
- Imagine your breath as a bridge between your inner self and the wordless forest around you.
- Practice this for 10-15 minutes, letting the tranquillity of the forest quiet your mind.

Conclusion

By embracing the wordless essence of who we are, we can find a profound sense of peace and connection within. In a world overflowing with words, taking the time to reconnect with our wordless inner selves through nature can help us regain clarity, tranquillity, and a deeper understanding of our true selves.

A butterfly, by the author

Chapter 14. Our Whole Selves

In the modern world, we are often forced to develop one specific aspect of our identity while ignoring the rest.

This usually happens at work, where we are slotted into a particular role and required to hone specific skills that the role demands, often at the expense of our other skills, abilities and feelings.

In the Office, Negative Space

Persisting in this narrow focus can lead to a skewed, exaggerated, and incomplete sense of self.

We become acutely aware of the one aspect of ourselves we constantly exercise at work, while forgetting about the other parts of ourselves that we have tucked away out of sight and out of mind. This imbalance can cause frustration, burnout, and a nagging sense of incompleteness.

The Bits of Self We Leave Behind

When we pour all our energy into professional excellence, we often leave behind various facets of our identity. Reconnecting with these parts can bring balance and fulfilment to our lives.

Let's explore these neglected parts and why it's crucial to rediscover them.

- **The Creative Self:** Remember when you used to love painting, writing stories, or playing an instrument? Creativity often takes a backseat in the pursuit of career goals, yet it is crucial for innovation and emotional well-being.

  If you've abandoned your creative hobbies, consider revisiting them. They can provide a much-needed break from work and provide a new way of sharing with others.

- **The Physical Self:** Think back to the days when you enjoyed playing sports, going for a run, or dancing without a care in the world. Our need for physical activity and the joy of moving our bodies can be neglected due to professional demands.

  Take regular exercise to boost your energy levels, improve your mood, and enhance your overall well-being.

- **The Emotional Self:** In a work-focused life, we may suppress our emotions to maintain professionalism, leading to emotional stagnation and stress.

  Allow yourself to feel and express your true emotions without leaving them bottled up inside you.

- **The Social Self:** Recall the times when you enjoyed spending hours talking with friends, attending social gatherings, or participating in community events. Networking for professional gain is not the same as fostering genuine connections. Meaningful relationships contribute to our sense of belonging and happiness.

  Reconnect with friends and family, join clubs or groups, and participate in social activities to enrich your life and provide a personal support system.

- **The Intellectual Self:** Remember the thrill of learning something new, whether it was a new language, a fascinating book, or an online course? Beyond the specific knowledge required for our job, there is a broader intellectual curiosity that encompasses diverse interests and lifelong learning.

    Make time to pursue intellectual interests outside of work to keep your mind sharp and inspired.

- **The Sensory Self:** Remember the simple pleasures of enjoying a delicious meal, listening to your favourite music, or experiencing the beauty of a sunset?

    Take time to savour sensory pleasures, whether it's cooking a gourmet meal, attending a concert, or simply enjoying the sights and sounds of nature.

Ice Cream, DALL-E

Nature as a Catalyst for Rediscovery

Nature provides the perfect backdrop for the process of self-rediscovery. The tranquillity and inspiration found in natural settings can help us reconnect with the parts of ourselves that we have neglected. The following mindfulness exercises can guide you on this journey.

Nature Reflection Walk

- Find a quiet, natural setting for a walk.
- As you walk, reflect on different aspects of your life and identity.
- Consider how each part contributes to your overall sense of self.

Creative Expression in Nature
- Bring a creative activity, such as drawing, writing, or playing music, into a natural setting.
- Let the environment inspire and inform your creative expression.

Conclusion

In a world that often demands we focus on specific aspects of ourselves, it is essential to take time to reconnect with our entire selves. Nature provides the perfect backdrop for this process, offering tranquillity and inspiration as we rediscover the parts of ourselves that make us complete.

Remember, the goal is not just professional excellence but rather complete and wholesome personal fulfilment. By taking the time to nurture all aspects of your identity, you can achieve a richer, more balanced, and ultimately more satisfying life.

Claude Monet Painting by the Edge of a Wood, John Singer Sargent

Chapter 15. The Natural Healing Ability of the Mind

Sometimes, we find ourselves in need of emotional healing for many and varied reasons. It could be the result of stress from work, personal loss, trauma, or simply the accumulation of everyday challenges. Emotional healing is essential for maintaining our overall well-being and quality of life.

There are various ways to accomplish this healing, including support from friends and family, engaging in hobbies and practicing mindfulness. However, one of the most powerful yet often overlooked methods is reconnecting with nature to strengthen our inherent capacity to heal.

Understanding the Mind's Healing Potential

Just as the human body has an incredible ability to heal itself - from mending broken bones to fighting infections, our minds have natural processes to deal with stress, recover from trauma, and regain emotional balance.

These processes can be hindered by artificial environments and the stresses of modern life. To activate and support the mind's healing capabilities, we can return to the place where the mind feels naturally whole and fresh, in the cradle of nature.

- **Immersion in Nature:** The sights, sounds, and smells of nature can calm the mind and enhance our sense of well-being. Whether it's a walk in the park, a hike in the mountains, or simply sitting in a garden, immersing ourselves in nature can provide a powerful balm for our troubled minds.

- **Mindful Practices:** Engaging in mindfulness and reflection helps us tune into our inner selves, fostering awareness and acceptance. This allows the mind to process and heal from emotional wounds.

- **Simplicity and Presence:** Embracing simplicity and being fully present in our daily activities can significantly reduce stress. By simplifying our lives and removing clutter, we create a mental environment that supports healing and growth.

Mindful Practices for Encouraging Natural Healing

The following practices can be used to deepen our connection to nature and encourage the mind to self-heal.

1. Healing Breath Reflection

1. Find a quiet, natural setting where you can sit comfortably.
2. Close your eyes and take slow, deep breaths, focusing on the sensation of the air entering and leaving your lungs.
3. With each inhale, imagine breathing in healing energy from the natural world around you.
4. With each exhale, release any tension or negative thoughts, allowing your mind to become lighter and more relaxed.
5. Continue this practice for 10-15 minutes, feeling the healing power of your breath and the natural environment.

2. Stream Cleansing Reflection

1. Find a comfortable place to sit by a stream or imagine one in your mind.
2. Close your eyes and focus on the sound of the water flowing gently over rocks.
3. Visualize the stream carrying away any negative thoughts or emotions, leaving your mind clear and refreshed.
4. Imagine the water infusing you with a sense of calm and renewal.
5. Spend 10-15 minutes in this practice, feeling the cleansing and healing effects of the stream.

3. Sunlight Nourishment Reflection

1. Sit in a sunny spot where you can feel the warmth of the sun on your skin.
2. Close your eyes and focus on the sensation of the sunlight touching your body.
3. Visualize the sunlight penetrating your skin and filling your entire being with healing energy and warmth.
4. Imagine this energy reaching every part of your mind, dissolving any tension or pain.

5. Practice for 10-15 minutes, absorbing the nourishing and healing power of the sunlight.

Conclusion

Just as the body naturally heals itself, the mind has an inherent capacity for healing and restoration. By reconnecting with nature we can encourage this natural propensity for mental and emotional healing.

Through mindful practices and a deeper connection to our true selves we can create an environment that supports the mind's natural healing processes and enhances our overall well-being.

Sunrise, by the author

Section III: The Health of the Natural World

In the ancient world, philosophers and thinkers believed that all matter was composed of four fundamental elements: fire, water, earth, and wind.

These elements were seen as the building blocks of the universe, each playing a crucial role in maintaining the balance and harmony of the natural world. This concept was seen not only a way to understand the physical world but also a framework for exploring the deeper connections between humans and nature.

In this section, we will explore how each of these ancient elements contributes to the health of the natural world and our own well-being.

Wind, Fire, Water, Earth, by the author

Chapter 17. Earth: The Richness of the Soil

The soil beneath our feet is a living, breathing entity that sustains nearly all life on Earth. It is the foundation of ecosystems, the source of our food, and a critical component of the planet's natural cycles.

By understanding and connecting with the soil, we can gain a deeper appreciation for the interconnectedness of life and find ways to reconnect with ourselves.

The Importance of Soil

Soil is often overlooked, yet it plays a vital role in the health of our planet and the well-being of all living organisms.

Here are some key aspects of soil's importance:

- **Foundation of Life:** Soil provides the essential nutrients that plants need to grow. These plants, in turn, support herbivores, which are prey for carnivores, forming the basis of food chains.

- **Nutrient Cycling:** Soil is a dynamic system that recycles nutrients through the decomposition of organic matter. This process enriches the soil and supports plant growth.

- **Water Filtration:** Soil acts as a natural filter, cleaning water as it percolates through the layers. This helps maintain clean groundwater and healthy aquatic ecosystems.

- **Carbon Storage:** Healthy soils store carbon, helping to mitigate climate change by reducing the amount of carbon dioxide in the atmosphere.

- **Habitat:** Soil is home to countless organisms, from bacteria and fungi to insects and earthworms, all of which contribute to its fertility and structure.

An earthworm, Dodo-Bird, Flickr

The Formation of Soil

Understanding the formation of soil can deepen our appreciation for this vital resource.

Soil is formed from the breakdown of rocks through a process called weathering. Over time, rocks are broken down into smaller and smaller particles by the effects of wind, water, and temperature changes. This physical weathering is complemented by chemical weathering, where minerals in the rocks are dissolved and transformed.

Plants growing in stones, Wikimedia Commons

As these rock particles continue to break down, organic material from decaying plants and animals is added to the mix. This organic matter enriches the soil with nutrients and helps retain moisture. Over time, layers of soil build up, creating a complex structure that supports plant life.

Earthworms and other soil organisms play a crucial role in maintaining the health of the soil. Earthworms, for example, aerate the soil by creating tunnels as they move through it. This aeration allows air and water to penetrate the soil more easily, promoting the growth of plants. Additionally, earthworms break down organic matter, turning it into nutrient-rich castings that further enhance soil fertility.

Connecting to the Soil

Connecting to the soil can give us a sense of stability and of being grounded. By engaging with the earth, we can tap into its richness and find a sense of balance and well-being.

Here are some ways to connect with the soil:

Gardening and Farming

Gardening and farming provide a profound and tactile way to connect with the soil. Imagine the feeling of your hands digging into the earth, the scent of freshly turned soil filling the air, and the sight of vibrant green shoots emerging from the ground.

When you plant a seed, you witness firsthand how the soil nurtures the seedling, providing it with the nutrients and stability it needs to grow. This hands-on experience teaches us patience and respect for nature's rhythms.

Gardening and farming also allow us to experience the rewards of our labour. The satisfaction of harvesting a ripe tomato or a fresh carrot, knowing that you played a part in its growth, is unparalleled. This direct interaction with the soil helps us appreciate its crucial role in sustaining life and deepens our connection to the natural world.

Carrot harvest, woodleywonderworks, Flickr

Barefoot Walking

Walking barefoot on the soil is a simple yet powerful practice that connects us to the earth in an intimate way. The sensation of the ground beneath our feet, whether it's soft grass, cool sand, or warm dirt, can be profoundly grounding.

Barefoot walking can also have significant physical benefits. The structure of the human foot is designed for barefoot walking. The foot consists of 26 bones, 33 joints, and over 100 muscles, tendons, and ligaments. This intricate design provides a remarkable combination of strength, flexibility, and sensory feedback, all of which are optimized for barefoot movement.

- **Stimulating Nerve Endings:** Walking barefoot stimulates the nerve endings in our feet, which enhances our sense of touch and proprioception—the awareness of our body's position and movement in space. This sensory feedback helps improve our balance and coordination.

- **Improving Balance and Posture:** Barefoot walking encourages a more natural gait and posture. When we walk barefoot, we tend to land on the mid-foot or forefoot rather than the heel, which is a more shock-absorbing and efficient way to walk.

    This natural gait reduces the impact on our joints and promotes better alignment of our spine and overall posture.

- **Promoting a Sense of Well-being:** The physical act of walking barefoot can also promote a sense of well-being. The increased sensory input from the ground beneath us can have a calming effect on the nervous system, helping to reduce stress and anxiety.

    Additionally, barefoot walking can help strengthen the muscles in our feet and lower legs, improving overall foot health and reducing the risk of injury.

Incorporating barefoot walking into your daily routine can be a simple yet profound way to reconnect with the earth and your natural self.

Start by walking barefoot in safe, natural environments, such as grassy fields, sandy beaches, or forest trails. Pay attention to the sensations under your feet and allow yourself to fully experience the grounding energy of the earth.

Planting

Planting a seedling can be a mindful practice that connects you with the cycle of life:

1. **Select a Plant:** Choose a small plant or seedling to plant in the soil.
2. **Prepare the Soil:** Dig a hole with your hands, feeling the earth's texture and structure.
3. **Plant with Intention:** Place the plant in the hole and cover it with soil. Focus on the act of giving life and nurturing growth. Reflect on the cycle of life and your role in it.
4. **Meditate on Connection:** Spend 10-15 minutes appreciating the connection between the soil, the plant, and yourself.

Conclusion

The soil is the foundation of life, supporting ecosystems and human civilization. By appreciating the soil, we can ground ourselves, appreciate the interconnectedness of life, and find a deeper sense of balance and well-being. Through mindful practices and meditation, we can foster a greater appreciation for the richness of the earth and our place within it, leading to a more harmonious and sustainable relationship with the natural world.

As you explore these practices, remember that the act of reconnecting with the soil is not just about physical touch but also about mental and emotional engagement. Allow yourself to be fully present in these moments, and let the earth guide you to a place of healing and wholeness.

Chapter 18. Fire: The Wonder of Sunlight

Imagine the primordial nuclear fire within the heart of the sun. Here, immense heat and pressure fuse hydrogen atoms into helium, releasing vast amounts of energy.

This energy, in the form of sunlight, travels 93 million miles to reach Earth, where it becomes the driving force behind one of the most miraculous processes on our planet: photosynthesis.

Sunlight enables plants to convert carbon dioxide and water into glucose, sustaining life by supporting plant growth and forming the foundation of the food chain.

The Sun; Wikimedia Commons

This amazing transformation that is performed by every green plant provides food and energy for all living organisms.

By understanding and appreciating sunlight and photosynthesis, we can deepen our connection to nature and recognize the intricate web of life that these processes support.

Forest sunlight; Wikimedia Commons

The Lifeblood of Nature

Photosynthesis is the process by which green plants, algae, and some bacteria convert light energy, usually from the sun, into chemical energy stored in molecules of glucose. Here's a brief overview of how it works:

- **Light Absorption:** Chlorophyll, the green pigment in plants, absorbs sunlight, primarily in the blue and red wavelengths.
- **Water Splitting:** The absorbed light energy is used to split water molecules (H_2O) into oxygen (O_2), protons (H+), and electrons (e-).
- **Energy Conversion:** The electrons and protons are used to convert carbon dioxide (CO_2) from the air into glucose ($C_6H_{12}O_6$), a type of sugar that provides energy for the plant.
- **Oxygen Release:** As a byproduct of photosynthesis, oxygen is released into the atmosphere, which is essential for the respiration of most living organisms.

This process can be summarized by the following equation:

$6CO_2 + 6H_2O + \text{light energy} \rightarrow C_6H_{12}O_6 + 6O_2$

Photosynthesis is the basis of life on Earth, supporting plants and, through them, all other organisms. In addition to food, it also provides the oxygen in the air that we breathe.

Photosynthesis and Global Warming

One of the critical roles of photosynthesis is its impact on the Earth's carbon cycle.

Plants absorb carbon dioxide (CO_2) from the atmosphere during photosynthesis and use it to produce glucose. This absorption of CO_2 helps regulate atmospheric levels of this greenhouse gas, which is crucial in preventing the buildup of CO_2 that leads to global warming.

Through photosynthesis, plants act as natural carbon sinks, storing carbon in their biomass and in the soil. This process of carbon sequestration is vital in mitigating the effects of climate change by reducing the amount of CO_2 in the atmosphere.

Mindfulness Exercises

Practicing mindfulness with a focus on sunlight and photosynthesis can help deepen our connection to these vital processes and the natural world.

Here are five meditation exercises to help you connect with the wonder of sunlight and photosynthesis:

Sunlight Absorption Reflection
1. Find a sunny spot outdoors where you can sit comfortably.
2. Close your eyes and feel the warmth of the sunlight on your skin.
3. Imagine that, like a plant, you are absorbing the sunlight, and visualize the light energy entering your body and spreading throughout.
4. Reflect on the process of photosynthesis and how sunlight is transformed into energy and life.
5. Meditate for 10-15 minutes, feeling connected to the energy of the sun and the natural world.

Note: Our bodies also absorb sunlight to create vitamin D, which is vital for bone health, immune function, and overall well-being.

Leaf Observation Reflection
1. Choose a green leaf from a plant or tree and hold it in your hand.
2. Examine the leaf closely, observing its veins, color, and texture.
3. Reflect on the role of the leaf in photosynthesis, capturing sunlight and converting it into energy.
4. Close your eyes and visualize the process of photosynthesis occurring within the leaf.
5. Meditate for 10-15 minutes, appreciating the intricate work of nature within the leaf.

Breath of Life Reflection
1. Sit comfortably in a natural setting, surrounded by plants.
2. Close your eyes and take slow, deep breaths, inhaling the oxygen produced by the plants around you.
3. With each inhale, imagine the oxygen entering your body and nourishing your cells.

4. With each exhale, release carbon dioxide, visualizing the plants absorbing it for photosynthesis.
5. Meditate for 10-15 minutes, feeling a sense of unity and reciprocity with the plant life around you.

Growth Visualization Reflection
1. Find a comfortable place to sit in your garden or a park.
2. Close your eyes and imagine a seed sprouting and growing into a plant.
3. Visualize the plant absorbing sunlight, taking in water and nutrients from the soil, and growing taller and stronger.
4. Reflect on the energy transformation happening through photosynthesis, fuelling the plant's growth.
5. Meditate for 10-15 minutes, feeling a connection to the growth and energy of plants.

Energy Flow Reflection
1. Sit or lie down in a place where you can see the sunlight filtering through leaves.
2. Focus on the dappled light and the way it moves through the leaves.
3. Imagine the light being captured by the leaves and converted into energy through photosynthesis.
4. Visualize this energy flowing through the plant, supporting its growth and vitality.
5. Meditate for 10-15 minutes, appreciating the continuous flow of energy from the sun to the plants and beyond.

Conclusion

Sunlight enables the miraculous process of photosynthesis that sustains life on Earth by providing glucose (sugar) for us to eat and oxygen for us to breath. This process also reduces the amount of carbon dioxide in the atmosphere, which reduces the effects of global warming.

By understanding and appreciating this process, we can develop a deeper connection to the natural world and recognize the intricate web of life that it supports.

Chapter 19. Water: Rain and Renewal

Rain is one of nature's most essential and awe-inspiring phenomena. It brings life to the earth, nourishes plants, replenishes water sources, and cleanses the air we breathe. From gentle drizzles to dramatic thunderstorms, rain takes many forms, each contributing to the health and vitality of our planet. By appreciating the wonder of rain, we can deepen our connection to the natural world and recognize its vital role in sustaining life.

Rain; rawpixel.com

The Life-Giving Power of Rain

Rain plays a crucial role in maintaining the balance of ecosystems and supporting life on Earth. Here are some key aspects of rain's importance:

- **Nourishment for Plants:** Rain provides the water that plants need to grow. It infiltrates the soil, reaching plant roots and enabling essential processes like photosynthesis.
- **Replenishing Water Sources:** Rainfall refills rivers, lakes, and aquifers, ensuring a continuous supply of fresh water for drinking, irrigation, and sanitation.

- **Cleansing the Air:** Rain helps to cleanse the atmosphere by washing away pollutants and dust particles, leading to cleaner air and improved health for living organisms.
- **Supporting Ecosystems:** Rain supports diverse ecosystems, from rainforests to wetlands, creating habitats for countless species of plants and animals.

The Role of Clouds

Clouds play a significant role in the water cycle and in regulating the Earth's climate. They are formed from the condensation of water vapor in the atmosphere, and they serve multiple essential functions:

- **Providing Water:** Clouds are the source of rain, snow, sleet, and hail. They transport water from the oceans and other bodies of water to different parts of the world, allowing plants to grow far from the source of the clouds in the ocean.
- **Reflecting Sunlight:** Clouds reflect some of the sun's sunlight back into space, which helps to prevent the Earth from overheating. This reflection, known as the albedo effect, is crucial in maintaining the planet's temperature balance and mitigating the effects of global warming.
- **Moderating Temperature:** Clouds moderate the Earth's temperature by trapping heat. During the day, they reflect sunlight and keep the world cooler, while at night, they trap heat and prevent it from escaping into space, stopping the temperature from getting too cold.

Clouds; pexel.com

Mindfulness Exercises for Connecting with Rain

Practicing meditation with a focus on rain can deepen our connection to this life-giving phenomenon and help us appreciate its role in sustaining the natural world. Here are five meditation exercises to help you connect with the wonder of rain:

Raindrop Reflection

- Sit comfortably near a window or outside where you can hear and see the rain.
- Close your eyes and focus on the sound of the raindrops, letting the rhythm of the rain calm your mind.
- Visualize each raindrop as a life-giving force, nourishing the earth and cleansing the air.
- Spend 10-15 minutes in this meditation, feeling the soothing presence of the rain.

Rain Walk Reflection

- Dress appropriately and take a slow, mindful walk in the rain.
- Focus on the sensation of the raindrops on your skin and the sound of the rain around you.
- Breathe deeply, inhaling the fresh, cleansed air, and exhaling any tension or stress.
- Meditate for 10-15 minutes, feeling a deep connection to the natural cycle of rain and renewal.

Water Cycle Reflection

- Sit comfortably and close your eyes.
- Visualize the water cycle: evaporation from oceans and lakes, condensation into clouds, and precipitation as rain.
- Imagine the rain falling on the earth, nourishing plants, replenishing water sources, and cleansing the air.
- Reflect on the continuous cycle of water and its vital role in sustaining life.
- Meditate for 10-15 minutes, appreciating the interconnectedness of the water cycle.

Thunderstorm Reflection

- If safe, sit near a window or outside under shelter during a thunderstorm.
- Close your eyes and focus on the sounds of the thunder and the intensity of the rain.
- Visualize the powerful energy of the storm cleansing and renewing the environment.
- Reflect on the dramatic impact of thunderstorms on the landscape and their role in nature's balance.
- Meditate for 10-15 minutes, feeling the awe and power of the storm.

Stream Reflection

- Sit near a stream or river that is rushing along after a rain.
- Listen to the sound of the water flowing, and focus on the significance of the water's journey from rain to river.
- Visualize how the rainwater nourishes plants, replenishes soil, and supports life along its path.
- Meditate for 10-15 minutes, appreciating the value and sustainability of this natural water cycle.

Conclusion

Rain is a miraculous and essential natural phenomenon that sustains life, nourishes plants, replenishes water sources, and cleanses the air.

By understanding and appreciating the benefits of rain, we can develop a deeper connection to the natural world and recognize its vital role in sustaining life.

Ouareau River after rain; Wikimedia Commons

Chapter 20. Wind: The Breath of Life

Wind is one of the most powerful and dynamic forces in nature. It shapes the landscape, influences weather patterns, and carries seeds and pollen that enable life to flourish.

Wind can be a gentle breeze that soothes our senses or a powerful gale that demonstrates the raw power of the natural world. By connecting with the wind, we can find a sense of freedom and renewal, as well as a deeper connection to the rhythms of nature.

The Gale; Antonio Parreiras, Creazilla

The Vital Role of Wind

Wind plays a crucial role in maintaining the balance of ecosystems and supporting life on Earth. Here are some key aspects of wind's importance:

- **Pollination and Seed Dispersal:** Wind helps plants reproduce by carrying pollen from one flower to another and spreading seeds over wide areas.
- **Weather and Climate:** Wind influences weather patterns and helps distribute heat and moisture around the planet, contributing to the regulation of climate.

- **Erosion and Landscape Formation:** Wind shapes the landscape by eroding rocks and soil, creating unique landforms such as dunes and canyons.
- **Oxygen Distribution:** Wind aids in the distribution of oxygen, ensuring that all living organisms have access to this vital element.

Forms of Wind

Wind has various forms, each with its unique character and impact on the environment:

- **Gentle Breezes:** Light, refreshing breezes provide comfort and carry the scents of nature, such as blooming flowers and fresh grass.
- **Steady Winds:** Moderate winds help ventilate the atmosphere, dispersing pollutants and bringing fresh air.
- **Gusty Winds:** Sudden, strong gusts can clear away debris and open up new spaces for growth and renewal.
- **Stormy Gales:** Powerful winds during storms demonstrate nature's strength and can reshape the landscape.

Mindfulness Exercises for Connecting with the Wind

Practicing meditation with a focus on the wind can deepen our connection to this powerful force and help us appreciate its role in sustaining the natural world. Here are five new meditation exercises to help you connect with the wonder of wind.

Breeze Sensation Reflection

- Find a quiet spot outdoors where you can sit comfortably and feel the breeze.
- Close your eyes and take slow, deep breaths, focusing on the sensation of the breeze on your skin.
- Imagine the breeze carrying away any stress or tension, leaving you feeling refreshed and light.
- Reflect on the gentle power of the wind and its role in nature.
- Meditate for 10-15 minutes, embracing the soothing presence of the breeze.

Wind Sound Reflection

- Sit in a place where you can hear the wind moving through trees, grass, or other natural elements.
- Close your eyes and focus on the sounds of the wind, letting them fill your mind.
- Imagine the wind as a voice of nature, speaking to you in a language of whispers and rustles.
- Reflect on the messages the wind might be conveying about change and renewal.
- Spend 10-15 minutes in this meditation, allowing the sounds of the wind to bring you peace and clarity.

Wind Dancing Reflection

- Stand in an open area where you can move freely, such as a meadow or beach.
- Close your eyes and feel the wind moving around you.
- Begin to sway and move your body in response to the wind, letting it guide your movements.
- Imagine that you are dancing with the wind, feeling a sense of freedom and connection to the natural world.
- Meditate for 10-15 minutes, enjoying the playful and liberating experience of wind dancing.

Wind Visualization Reflection

- Find a comfortable place to sit where you can feel the wind or imagine it vividly.
- Close your eyes and visualize the wind as a flowing energy, moving around and through you.
- Picture the wind carrying away any negative thoughts or emotions, leaving you feeling clear and light.
- Reflect on the cleansing and renewing power of the wind.
- Spend 10-15 minutes in this meditation, feeling a deep connection to the wind's energy.

Breath of Life Reflection

- Sit comfortably outdoors or near an open window where you can feel the wind.
- Close your eyes and synchronize your breath with the rhythm of the wind, inhaling and exhaling slowly.
- Imagine the wind as a breath of life, filling you with energy and vitality.
- Reflect on the interconnectedness of your breath and the wind, both essential for life.
- Meditate for 10-15 minutes, feeling a sense of unity with the natural world.

Conclusion

Wind is a powerful and essential force in nature that sustains life, shapes the landscape, and influences the climate. By understanding and appreciating the various forms and benefits of wind, we can develop a deeper connection to the natural world and recognize its vital role in sustaining life.

Embrace the wind as a source of inspiration and renewal, and let it guide you to greater appreciation for the beauty and dynamism of the natural world.

Wind Swept Trees in Winter, Wikimedia Commons

Section IV: The Five Senses

Our senses are the gateways to experiencing the world in its full richness and beauty. They connect us to our environment, evoke memories, and profoundly influence our emotions and well-being.

Modernity, however, with its synthetic stimuli and constant bombardment of artificial images, sounds, and smells, divorces us from the authentic, healthful sensing that the natural world provides. Instead, it offers us only a plastic representation of nature, such as artificial lighting, processed sounds and digital nature scenes, which offer a superficial connection that lacks the depth and complexity of genuine interactions with the natural world.

Engaging with our senses through natural experiences can bring a profound sense of calm, joy and mental clarity.

The Rose Garden; DALL E

Chapter 21. Introduction: Sensory Healing

Our senses are vital for experiencing the world in its full richness and beauty. They connect us to our environment, evoke memories, and profoundly influence our emotions and well-being.

In the past, people tuned into the sounds of the wind and water, the textures of the earth and plants, the flavours of natural foods, and the scents carried by the breeze. These natural sensory experiences were essential for maintaining balance within oneself and with the environment.

Today, our sensory experiences are often dominated by artificiality. Synthetic scents, processed foods, harsh lighting, and constant noise from urban environments can overwhelm and dull our senses. These commercial substitutes can never fully replicate the depth and authenticity of natural experiences.

We can benefit by substituting the artificial stimuli we are used to experiencing with their natural counterparts:

Sense	The Artificial Experience	The Natural Experience
Touch	We touch synthetic fabrics and plastics that lack the richness of the natural world.	Rediscover the pleasure of natural textures. Feel the coolness of a river stone, the roughness of tree bark, or the softness of moss.
Sight	Our visual environment is dominated by screens and artificial lighting, which can strain our eyes and prevent us experiencing the natural cycle of night and day.	Spend time in nature, letting your eyes rest on the green of leaves, the blue of the sky, or the myriad colors of a flower garden.

Sense	The Artificial Experience	The Natural Experience
Taste	Processed foods laden with artificial flavours and preservatives dull our taste buds and disconnect us from the fresh, vibrant flavours of natural, whole foods.	Embrace the flavours of fresh, whole foods. Savor the sweetness of a ripe berry, the zest of a fresh herb, or the crunch of a raw vegetable.
Smell	Synthetic fragrances in perfumes, cleaning products, and air fresheners overwhelm our sense of smell, masking the subtle and complex aromas of flowers, herbs, and other natural sources.	Inhale the scents of nature. Breathe in the fragrance of a blooming flower, the earthy smell of wet soil, or the crisp scent of pine needles.
Hearing	Constant noise from traffic, machinery, and electronic devices drown out the calming and restorative sounds of nature.	Listen to the sounds of nature. Find a quiet spot and tune in to the chirping of birds, the rustle of leaves, or the babbling of a brook.

This section of the book explores how to reawaken and nurture our senses through mindful engagement with nature. We will delve into each sense—smell, touch, hearing, sight, and taste—and discover practical ways to integrate natural sensory experiences into our daily lives, even in urban environments.

By embracing sensory healing, we can enhance our connection to nature, enrich our daily experiences, and improve our overall well-being.

Chapter 22. Smell

The sense of smell holds a profound and intimate connection to the human experience.

Unlike our other senses, the olfactory system has a direct line to the brain's limbic system, the area responsible for emotions and memories. This unique pathway allows scents to evoke vivid memories and deep emotions.

The Olfactory Journey: From Nose to Memory

When you inhale, odour molecules travel through the nasal passages to the olfactory receptors located at the top of the nasal cavity. These receptors send signals directly to the olfactory bulb in the brain, which then transmits information to the limbic system. This is the same region that governs emotional responses and memory formation. Thus, a simple whiff of a particular scent can trigger a cascade of emotions and recollections.

Imagine walking down a dusty road after a rainstorm. The distinctive scent of rain on dry earth fills the air. Suddenly, you are transported back to a summer day decades ago, playing in the yard with your childhood friends.

The power of scent lies in its ability to unlock memories buried deep within your subconscious, bringing them to the forefront of your mind with remarkable clarity.

Glen Callater; Wikimedia Commons

The Emotional Landscape of Smell

The sense of smell can evoke a wide range of emotions, for instance:

- **Comfort and Security**: The smell of freshly baked bread might remind you of your grandmother's kitchen, evoking feelings of warmth and security.

- **Nostalgia**: The scent of a particular flower, like jasmine or rose, can take you back to a specific place and time, evoking a sense of nostalgia.

- **Joy and Excitement**: The aroma of a favourite dish cooking in the kitchen can bring about a sense of anticipation and joy.

These emotional responses are powerful because they are tied to personal experiences. Each scent carries with it a unique set of memories and feelings, creating a rich tapestry of sensory experiences.

The Modern Challenge: Smell in Urban Environments

In modern, urbanized environments, our sense of smell is often drowned out by artificial odours and pollutants.

The constant presence of exhaust fumes, industrial emissions, and synthetic fragrances can overwhelm our olfactory senses, making it challenging to experience the subtle and natural scents of the environment.

This sensory overload can desensitize us to the rich tapestry of smells that the natural world offers, leading to a diminished appreciation for the olfactory dimension of our experiences.

Cultivating a Deeper Connection with Smell

In our modern, often visually and auditorily overstimulated world, we may overlook the subtleties of our olfactory experiences. By paying closer attention to the scents around us, we can cultivate a deeper connection to our environment and our own inner experiences. Here are a few ways to enhance your sense of smell and its impact on your life:

- **Mindful Smelling**: Take moments throughout your day to consciously inhale and appreciate the natural scents around you. Whether it's the aroma of your morning coffee, the fresh air after a rain, or the scent of a blooming flower, be present and mindful of these experiences.

- **Scent Journaling**: Keep a journal of different scents you encounter and the memories or emotions they evoke. This practice can help you become more attuned to your olfactory experiences and the personal significance they hold.
- **Aromatherapy**: Utilize essential oils and aromatic plants to enhance your well-being. Scents like lavender, rosemary, and eucalyptus can have calming, invigorating, or purifying effects.

Conclusion

The sense of smell is a gateway to the past, a trigger for emotions, and a vital part of our daily existence.

By embracing the depth and richness of our olfactory experiences, we can enhance our connection to the world around us and to our own personal histories.

In the following chapter, we will explore how you can bring the natural smells of plants into your urban environment, creating a sensory oasis that enriches your life and connects you to the profound power of natural scent.

Frankincense Tree, Wikimedia Commons

Chapter 23. Bringing Aromatic Nature Indoors

Connecting to nature in the city through the natural smell of plants can be a refreshing way to bring the outdoors into urban living. Certain plants are particularly suitable for this purpose due to their aromatic qualities and ability to thrive in various urban environments.

Here are some plants that you can use to connect with nature in the city through the sense of natural smells.

Lavender (*Lavandula*)
- **Benefits:** Known for its calming and relaxing scent, lavender can help reduce stress and anxiety.
- **How to Use:** Plant lavender in pots on balconies, window sills, or in small urban gardens. You can also place dried lavender sachets around your home.

Rosemary (*Rosmarinus officinalis*)
- **Benefits:** Rosemary has a refreshing, invigorating aroma that can improve concentration and boost mood.
- **How to Use:** Grow rosemary in pots or as part of an herb garden. Place potted rosemary near windows or in kitchen areas where you can easily access its scent.

Jasmine (*Jasminum*)
- **Benefits:** Jasmine flowers emit a sweet, romantic fragrance that can promote relaxation and improve sleep quality.
- **How to Use:** Plant jasmine in containers or let it climb trellises on balconies. Choose varieties suited for container growth.

Mint (*Mentha*)
- **Benefits:** Mint's strong, fresh scent can invigorate the senses and clear the mind.
- **How to Use:** Grow mint in pots, as it can spread aggressively. Place it in areas where you can easily brush against the leaves to release its fragrance.

Basil (*Ocimum basilicum*)
- **Benefits:** Basil has a sweet, spicy aroma that can be both uplifting and calming.
- **How to Use:** Plant basil in pots or small garden beds. It's perfect for kitchen windowsills where you can enjoy the scent while cooking.

Eucalyptus (*Eucalyptus*)
- **Benefits:** Eucalyptus leaves have a clean, menthol-like scent that is refreshing and purifying.
- **How to Use:** Grow eucalyptus in large pots or as small trees on balconies or terraces. You can also use cut eucalyptus branches indoors.

Lemon Balm (*Melissa officinalis*)
- **Benefits:** Lemon balm has a mild lemon scent that is calming and can help with anxiety and sleep.
- **How to Use:** Plant lemon balm in containers or garden beds. It's a great choice for patio gardens.

Geranium (*Pelargonium*)
- **Benefits:** Scented geraniums come in various fragrances, including rose, lemon, and mint. They are known for their pleasant and uplifting aromas.
- **How to Use:** Grow scented geraniums in pots or hanging baskets. Place them near seating areas where you can enjoy their scent.

Gardenia (*Gardenia jasminoides*)
- **Benefits:** Gardenias have a rich, sweet fragrance that is often used in perfumes and can create a soothing atmosphere.
- **How to Use:** Plant gardenias in pots or in garden beds. Ensure they get plenty of sunlight and well-drained soil.

Thyme (*Thymus*)
- **Benefits:** Thyme has a warm, herbaceous scent that can be both soothing and invigorating.
- **How to Use:** Grow thyme in pots or as ground cover in small gardens. Place it where you can easily touch it to release its fragrance.

Creating a Scent Garden

To maximize the benefits of aromatic plants in an urban setting, consider creating a scent garden:

- **Planter Boxes and Pots:** Use planter boxes and pots to grow a variety of aromatic plants. This allows for mobility and versatility in limited spaces.

- **Vertical Gardens:** Use vertical gardening techniques to grow plants on walls or fences, enhancing the use of space and accessibility.

- **Window Boxes:** Install window boxes to grow fragrant herbs and flowers. This not only improves air quality but also provides a pleasant aroma when windows are open.

- **Balcony and Patio Gardens:** Transform balconies and patios into green oases by incorporating a mix of aromatic plants in containers and hanging baskets.

By integrating these aromatic plants into your urban living space, you can create a sensory connection to nature, enhancing your environment with the natural scents and benefits of the outdoors, even in the heart of the city.

Eucalyptus Trees; Wikimedia Commons

Chapter 24. Touch

The sense of touch is a fundamental aspect of the human experience, deeply intertwined with our physical, emotional, and psychological well-being.

Consider the simple act of walking barefoot on a sandy beach. The sensation of sand grains slipping through your toes can instantly transport you to a memory of a cherished vacation or a carefree summer day. This immediate and evocative power of touch lies in its ability to connect us deeply with past experiences and emotions.

Unlike other senses, touch is not localized to a specific part of the body but is spread throughout, allowing us to interact with and perceive the world in a uniquely rich way.

The Journey of Touch: From Skin to Brain

When we touch something, sensory receptors in our skin send signals through the nervous system to the brain. These signals are processed in the somatosensory cortex, which interprets the information about texture, temperature, and pressure.

This process happens almost instantaneously, allowing us to respond quickly to our environment.

The Emotional Landscape of Touch

Touch is profoundly connected to our emotions and can evoke a wide range of feelings, from comfort and security to excitement and nostalgia. For example:

- **Comfort and Security**: A warm embrace from a loved one can create feelings of safety and belonging.
- **Excitement**: The touch of a breeze on a hot day or the feel of cool water can evoke a sense of joy and refreshment.
- **Nostalgia**: The texture of an old book or the feel of a familiar fabric can bring back memories of childhood or significant moments.

These emotional responses are powerful because they are deeply personal and tied to our individual experiences. Each tactile sensation carries a unique set of memories and feelings, enriching our sensory world.

The Timelessness of Touch

One of the most remarkable aspects of touch is its timelessness. It has the unique ability to bridge the past and present, allowing us to relive memories through sensory experiences. For instance, touching the smooth surface of a well-loved object can transport you back to another time and place, evoking the same emotions and sensations you felt years ago.

Imagine feeling the rough bark of a tree. This simple experience can suddenly take you back to your childhood, climbing trees and feeling a sense of adventure and freedom. The sense of touch creates a direct link between the present moment and past experiences, making memories vivid and alive again.

Tree Bark; Martin Vorel

The Role of Touch in Daily Life

Beyond evoking memories and emotions, the sense of touch plays a critical role in our daily lives. It helps us navigate our environment, perform tasks, and interact with others. Touch can enhance our experiences in various ways:

- **Navigation and Safety**: Tactile feedback helps us avoid hazards and manage our environment effectively.

- **Sensory Enjoyment**: The texture of food, the feel of different materials, and the sensation of comfortable clothes all contribute to our enjoyment of daily activities.

- **Social Interaction**: Touch is fundamental to human connection, from a handshake to a hug, facilitating communication and bonding.

The Modern Challenge: Touch in Urban Environments

In modern, urbanized environments, our sense of touch is often dulled by the prevalence of artificial materials and the lack of natural textures. Concrete, metal, and plastic dominate our surroundings, reducing opportunities for tactile engagement with the natural world.

This sensory deprivation can lead to a diminished appreciation for the tactile dimension of our experiences and a loss of connection to the calming and grounding effects of natural textures.

Cultivating a Deeper Connection with Touch

To counteract the sensory overload and artificiality of urban living, we can intentionally cultivate our sense of touch by incorporating natural materials and textures into our daily lives. Here are a few ways to enhance your tactile experiences and reconnect with the natural world:

- **Mindful Touch**: Take moments throughout your day to consciously engage with different natural textures around you. Whether it's the feel of a wooden table, the softness of a natural fabric, or the roughness of a stone, be present and mindful of these natural tactile experiences.

- **Tactile Journaling**: Keep a journal of different natural textures you encounter and the memories or emotions they evoke. This practice can help you become more attuned to your tactile experiences and their personal significance.

- **Nature Walks**: Spend time in nature, touching different plants, trees, and natural elements. Notice the variety of textures and how they make you feel.

Conclusion

The sense of touch is a gateway to the past, a trigger for emotions, and a vital part of our daily existence. By embracing the depth and richness of our tactile experiences, we can enhance our connection to the world around us and to our own personal histories.

In the following chapter, we will explore how you can bring the natural textures of plants and materials into your urban environment, creating a sensory oasis that enriches your life and connects you to the profound power of touch.

Chapter 25. Engaging with Nature Through Texture

Connecting to nature in the city through tactile experiences can significantly enhance your sensory awareness and bring a sense of calm and grounding to urban living.

Certain plants and materials are particularly suitable for this purpose due to their textures and ability to thrive in various urban environments. Here are some plants and materials you can use to connect with nature in the city through the sense of touch.

Textured Plants

Moss (*Bryophyta*)

- **Benefits**: Moss provides a soft, cushiony texture that is soothing to touch and can create a calming environment.
- **How to Use**: Grow moss in shaded areas, on stones, or as a ground cover in urban gardens. You can also create a moss garden in a container for indoor spaces.

Lamb's Ear (*Stachys byzantina*)

- **Benefits**: Lamb's Ear has velvety, soft leaves that are pleasant to touch and can bring a sense of comfort and relaxation.
- **How to Use**: Plant Lamb's Ear in pots or garden beds where you can easily access and touch the leaves.

Ornamental Grasses (*Poaceae*)

- **Benefits**: The feathery, swaying texture of ornamental grasses can provide a gentle tactile experience and add a dynamic element to urban spaces.
- **How to Use**: Grow ornamental grasses in containers, along pathways, or as part of a mixed border in urban gardens.

Ferns (*Polypodiopsida*)

- **Benefits**: Ferns have delicate, feathery fronds that can be softly brushed for a gentle tactile sensation.
- **How to Use**: Grow ferns in shaded areas, hanging baskets, or as part of a vertical garden.

Herbs with Textured Leaves (*Various*)

- **Sage (Salvia officinalis)**: Soft, fuzzy leaves that provide a calming tactile experience.
- **Thyme (Thymus)**: Small, fine leaves that can be gently brushed for a soothing touch.
- **How to Use**: Grow these herbs in pots or small garden beds, particularly in kitchen areas where you can easily access and touch them.

Tree Bark (Various)

- **Benefits**: The rough, textured surface of tree bark can provide a grounding tactile experience and connect you to nature's sturdiness.
- **How to Use**: Plant small trees with interesting bark textures, such as birch or cedar, in urban gardens or large pots on balconies.

Textured Materials

Wooden Elements

- **Benefits**: Natural wood surfaces offer a warm, comforting texture that can be grounding and soothing.
- **How to Use**: Incorporate wooden benches, planters, and walkways into your urban garden or balcony space.

Stone and Pebbles

- **Benefits**: Smooth pebbles and rough stones can provide varied tactile experiences that are both calming and grounding.
- **How to Use**: Create a pebble pathway, add stone elements to garden beds, or use pebbles in potted plants.

Water Features

- **Benefits**: The feel of water, whether from a fountain or a small pond, can provide a refreshing and soothing tactile experience.
- **How to Use**: Install a small water feature on your balcony or patio, or use a tabletop fountain indoors.

Creating a Tactile Garden

To maximize the benefits of tactile experiences in an urban setting, consider creating a tactile garden:

- **Planter Boxes and Pots**: Use planter boxes and pots to grow a variety of plants with interesting textures. This allows for mobility and versatility in limited spaces.

- **Vertical Gardens**: Use vertical gardening techniques to grow textured plants on walls or fences, enhancing the use of space and accessibility.

- **Window Boxes**: Install window boxes to grow herbs and plants with interesting leaves. This provides a pleasant tactile experience when windows are open.

- **Balcony and Patio Gardens**: Transform balconies and patios into tactile oases by incorporating a mix of textured plants in containers and hanging baskets.

- **Tactile Pathways**: Create pathways using smooth pebbles, rough stones, or wooden planks to enhance the tactile experience as you walk through your garden.

By integrating these tactile elements into your urban living space, you can create a sensory connection to nature, enhancing your environment with the natural textures and benefits of the outdoors, even in the heart of the city.

Moss; the author

Chapter 26. Hearing

The sense of hearing is an essential and intricate part of the human experience, deeply connected to our emotions, memories, and communication.

Consider the simple act of listening to the rustling of leaves in a forest. The gentle sound can instantly transport you to a serene memory of a peaceful walk in the woods, bringing with it a sense of calm and connection to nature. This immediate and evocative power of hearing lies in its ability to connect us deeply with past experiences and emotions.

Hearing allows us to perceive the world in a dynamic way, picking up on sounds that can alert us to danger, bring us joy, or connect us to others.

The Journey of Sound: From Ear to Brain

When we hear a sound, vibrations travel through the air and enter our ears. These vibrations pass through the outer ear to the eardrum, causing it to vibrate. The vibrations are then transmitted to the inner ear, where they are converted into electrical signals by tiny hair cells in the cochlea. These signals travel along the auditory nerve to the brain, where they are interpreted as sounds in the auditory cortex.

The Emotional Landscape of Hearing

Hearing is deeply intertwined with our emotions and can evoke a wide range of feelings, from joy and comfort to nostalgia and sadness. For example:

- **Comfort and Security:** The soothing sound of a loved one's voice or a lullaby can create feelings of safety and comfort.
- **Joy and Excitement:** The upbeat rhythm of a favourite song or the cheerful chirping of birds can evoke a sense of happiness and energy.
- **Nostalgia:** The sound of a specific tune, like a childhood song or a distant train whistle, can bring back memories of significant moments.

These emotional responses are powerful because they are deeply personal and tied to our individual experiences. Each sound carries a unique set of memories and feelings, enriching our sensory world.

The Primal Sounds of Nature

Natural sounds have a primal richness that artificial noises often lack. The sounds of nature—such as the whispering of the wind through trees, the gentle murmur of a flowing stream, or the melodic calls of birds—resonate deeply within us. These sounds are inherently soothing and grounding, connecting us to the earth and to our primal instincts.

- **Wind in the Trees:** The sound of the wind rustling through leaves can evoke a sense of peace and timelessness, reminding us of our connection to the natural world.

- **Flowing Water:** The gentle babble of a brook or the rhythmic crashing of ocean waves can create a meditative state, reducing stress and promoting relaxation.

- **Birdsong:** The varied and melodious calls of birds can uplift our spirits, providing a sense of joy and connection to nature.

A finch in song; PxHere.com

These natural sounds are often absent or drowned out in urban environments, where the constant noise of traffic, construction, and human activity can overwhelm our senses. The chatter of suburbia, with its honking cars, blaring sirens, and the hum of machinery, lacks the depth and emotional resonance of natural sounds.

Cultivating a Deeper Connection with Hearing

To counteract the sensory overload and artificiality of urban living, we can intentionally cultivate our sense of hearing by seeking out natural sounds and creating environments that support auditory mindfulness. Here are a few ways to enhance your auditory experiences and reconnect with the natural world:

- **Mindful Listening:** Take moments throughout your day to consciously listen to the sounds around you. Whether it's the rustling of leaves, the chirping of birds, or the patter of rain, be present and mindful of these auditory experiences.
- **Soundscapes:** Create soundscapes in your living space by incorporating natural sounds, such as recordings of ocean waves, forest ambiances, or gentle rain. These can help reduce stress and improve focus.
- **Nature Walks:** Spend time in nature, paying attention to the diverse sounds. Notice the variety of bird calls, the rustling of leaves, and the flow of water. Allow these natural sounds to soothe and rejuvenate you.

Conclusion

The sense of hearing is a gateway to the past, a trigger for emotions, and a vital part of our daily existence. By embracing the depth and richness of our auditory experiences, we can enhance our connection to the world around us and to our own personal histories.

In the following chapter, we will explore how you can bring the natural sounds of the environment into your urban living space, creating a sensory oasis that enriches your life and connects you to the profound power of hearing.

Dynjandi Waterfalls, Iceland; Wikimedia Commons

Chapter 27. Creating a Natural Symphony in the City

Living in a city often means being surrounded by constant noise and artificial sounds, which can overwhelm our senses and create stress.

However, it is possible to create a natural auditory environment that brings a sense of calm and grounding to urban living. By integrating elements and practices that produce soothing natural sounds, you can enhance your sensory awareness and reconnect with nature, even in the heart of the city.

Here are some effective ways to create a natural symphony in your urban space.

Natural Sound Features

Bird Feeders and Birdbaths

- **Benefits:** Attracting birds to your urban space can fill your environment with the melodic sounds of bird songs, providing a natural and soothing auditory experience. Birds bring a dynamic element to your surroundings, with their songs changing throughout the day and season, adding a layer of richness to your auditory landscape.

- **How to Use:** Place bird feeders and birdbaths on balconies, in gardens, or on window sills. Choose feeders that attract a variety of local bird species to ensure a diverse range of bird songs. Keep the feeders clean and filled with appropriate birdseed to encourage frequent visits. Birdbaths should be refreshed regularly to provide a reliable water source.

Water Features

- **Benefits:** The sound of flowing water can create a calming and meditative atmosphere, helping to drown out urban noise and bring a sense of peace. Water features can mimic the sounds of streams or rivers, adding a tranquil element to your space.

- **How to Use:** Install a small fountain, waterfall, or tabletop water feature on your balcony, patio, or even inside your home. Ensure the water feature is placed in an area where you can easily hear its soothing sounds. For an added natural touch, surround the water feature with plants to create a mini oasis.

Wind Chimes

- **Benefits:** Wind chimes produce gentle, melodic sounds that can create a relaxing and tranquil environment, enhancing your connection to the natural elements. The sound of wind chimes can be particularly effective in masking urban noise and creating a peaceful ambiance.

- **How to Use:** Hang wind chimes in areas where they can catch the breeze, such as balconies, patios, or near open windows. Choose wind chimes made from natural materials like bamboo or metal for a more organic sound. Experiment with different types of chimes to find the tones that resonate best with you.

Potted Plants with Rustling Leaves

- **Benefits:** Certain plants have leaves that produce a pleasant rustling sound when moved by the wind, adding a natural auditory element to your urban space. This rustling sound can evoke a sense of being in a forest or a meadow, helping you feel more connected to nature.

- **How to Use:** Grow plants like bamboo, ornamental grasses, or small trees in pots on your balcony or patio. Place them where they can catch the wind and create a soothing rustling sound. Group plants together to amplify the rustling effect and create a mini forest vibe.

Creating an Urban Natural Symphony

By integrating these elements into your urban living space, you can create a natural symphony that brings the soothing sounds of nature into your daily life. Here are some additional tips to enhance your auditory connection to nature:

- **Nature Sound Recordings:** Use recordings of natural sounds, such as rain, ocean waves, or forest ambiances, to create a relaxing soundscape in your home. Play these sounds during meditation, relaxation, or even while working to reduce stress and improve focus.

- **Mindful Listening Practices:** Take time each day to practice mindful listening. Sit quietly and focus on the natural sounds around you, whether it's the birds singing, the wind rustling through leaves, or the gentle trickle of a water feature. This practice can help you develop a deeper appreciation for the subtle sounds of nature.

- **Outdoor Retreats:** Whenever possible, spend time in natural settings outside the city. Visit parks, gardens, or nature reserves to immerse yourself in the full spectrum of natural sounds. These experiences can rejuvenate your senses and provide a respite from the urban noise.

Conclusion

The sense of hearing is a vital part of our daily existence, connecting us to our environment and enriching our experiences.

By creating a natural symphony in the city, you can enhance your connection to nature and improve your overall well-being. Embrace the soothing sounds of birds, water, wind, and rustling leaves to transform your urban space into a sanctuary of calm and tranquillity.

Blue Jays in a Birdbath; Mike's Birds, Flickr

Chapter 28. Sight

The sense of sight is one of the most powerful and vital senses, deeply intertwined with our perception of the world, our emotions, and our cognitive processes. Sight allows us to navigate our environment, appreciate beauty, and connect with others through visual cues.

Consider the simple act of watching a sunset. The gradual change of colors in the sky can evoke a sense of awe and tranquillity, transporting you to a memory of a perfect day spent in nature. This immediate and evocative power of sight lies in its ability to connect us deeply with our surroundings and past experiences.

Sunset; the author

The Journey of Light: From Eye to Brain

When we see something, light enters our eyes through the cornea and lens, which focus the light onto the retina at the back of the eye. The retina contains photoreceptor cells that convert light into electrical signals. These signals travel along the optic nerve to the brain, where they are processed in the visual cortex.

This intricate process happens almost instantaneously, allowing us to perceive the world in rich detail and vibrant color.

The Emotional Landscape of Sight

The sense of sight is profoundly connected to our emotions and can evoke a wide range of feelings, from joy and wonder to nostalgia and peace. For example:

- **Joy and Wonder:** The sight of a blooming garden or a breathtaking landscape can fill us with happiness and awe.
- **Nostalgia:** Seeing a familiar place or an old photograph can bring back memories of significant moments in our lives.
- **Peace and Tranquillity:** Observing a calm lake or a gentle snowfall can create a sense of serenity and relaxation.

These emotional responses are powerful because they are deeply personal and tied to our individual experiences.

Visual Strain in Urban Environments

In modern, urban environments, our sense of sight is challenged by the artificial surroundings we live in. The constant presence of tall buildings, narrow streets, and dense cityscapes restricts our ability to see into the distance and appreciate expansive views. In contrast, looking out over a wide expanse of countryside and sky can have a liberating effect, broadening our minds and opening our hearts to new possibilities.

A lighthouse; the author

In addition, artificial environments can be visually jarring due to harsh lighting, repetitive patterns, and lack of natural elements. This can lead to visual fatigue and stress.

Natural environments, on the other hand, tend to be soothing to the eye. The organic shapes, diverse colors, and natural lighting found in nature provide a calming visual experience. Our eyes are naturally adapted to these settings, which help reduce strain and promote relaxation.

Cultivating a Deeper Connection with Sight

To counteract the visual constraints of urban living, we can intentionally cultivate our sense of sight by seeking out and creating opportunities to experience natural vistas.

Here are a few ways to enhance your visual experiences and reconnect with the natural world, even while in the city.

- **Visit Parks and Green Spaces:** Spend time in local parks, botanical gardens, or nature reserves. Find spots with expansive views, such as hilltops or lakesides, where you can take in the natural scenery.

- **Create Visual Access Points:** If possible, arrange your living or working space to have views of nature. Position seating areas near windows with views of gardens, trees, or distant horizons.

- **Take Scenic Routes:** When traveling through the city, choose routes that offer glimpses of natural beauty, such as riverside paths, tree-lined streets, or urban parks. These brief visual breaks can refresh your mind and spirit.

- **Practice Visual Mindfulness:** Take moments throughout your day to consciously observe your surroundings. Look for natural elements, even in urban settings, such as patches of sky between buildings, the play of light and shadow, or the movement of clouds.

Conclusion

The sense of sight is a gateway to the world, a trigger for emotions, and a vital part of our daily existence. By embracing the depth and richness of our visual experiences, we can enhance our connection to the world around us and to our own personal histories. In the following chapter, we will explore how you can create a visual connection to nature in your urban environment, broadening your horizons and opening your mind to the beauty and serenity of the natural world.

Chapter 29. Urban Spaces with Natural Views

Connecting to nature in the city through visual experiences can significantly enhance your sensory awareness and bring a sense of calm and openness to urban living.

Despite the constraints of urban environments, there are various ways to create natural viewing experiences that allow you to enjoy the beauty and serenity of nature.

Creating a Natural Viewing Experience in the City

Here are some strategies to connect with nature in the city through visual elements.

Window Gardens and Indoor Plants

- **Benefits**: Bringing greenery into your home through window gardens and indoor plants can create a refreshing and calming visual environment.
- **How to Use**: Place potted plants on windowsills, balconies, or in well-lit areas of your home. Choose a variety of plants with different shapes, colors, and sizes to create a visually stimulating display.

Vertical Gardens and Green Walls

- **Benefits**: Vertical gardens and green walls maximize limited space and add a lush, natural element to urban environments.
- **How to Use**: Install vertical gardens on balconies, patios, or indoor walls. Use modular systems or DIY setups to grow a variety of plants, including herbs, flowers, and foliage.

Balcony and Rooftop Gardens

- **Benefits**: Transforming balconies and rooftops into green spaces provides a personal retreat with natural views.
- **How to Use**: Grow a variety of plants in containers, including flowers, herbs, and small shrubs. Arrange seating areas to face the greenery, creating a relaxing spot to enjoy the view.

Bird Feeders and Wildlife Attractions

- **Benefits**: Attracting birds and other wildlife to your space can add dynamic and engaging visual elements to your environment.

- **How to Use**: Install bird feeders, birdbaths, and nesting boxes on balconies or in gardens. Choose native plants that attract butterflies, bees, and other pollinators to create a lively and diverse visual experience.

Sky Watching and Natural Light

- **Benefits**: Observing the sky and maximizing natural light can enhance your connection to the natural world and improve your mood.

- **How to Use**: Arrange seating areas to face windows or open spaces where you can watch the sky, clouds, and stars. Keep curtains open during the day to let in natural light, and use mirrors to reflect light and brighten your space.

Creating an Illusion of Expanse

Even in a relatively small planting space, you can create the illusion of being in a large natural environment by cleverly arranging plants to screen everything beyond them. Here are some tips to achieve this effect:

- **Layering Plants**: Arrange plants of varying heights and densities to create depth and visual interest. Use taller plants or trees at the back and gradually transition to shorter plants in the front. This layered effect can make your space feel larger and more immersive.

- **Using Trellises and Arbours**: Incorporate trellises, arbours, or pergolas to support climbing plants and create vertical green walls. These structures can block unsightly views and give the impression of being surrounded by nature.

- **Creating Natural Screens**: Use dense foliage plants or hedges to form natural screens. Bamboo, tall grasses, and evergreen shrubs are excellent choices for creating privacy and a sense of enclosure.

- **Strategic Plant Placement**: Position plants to frame the best views and hide undesirable elements. Place larger plants or trees strategically to block urban clutter while drawing attention to natural features.

- **Mirrors and Reflective Surfaces**: Use mirrors or reflective surfaces to visually expand the space. Position them to reflect greenery and sky, creating an illusion of a larger, more open area.

Additionally, to create an increased sense of depth and perspective in your garden, consider these techniques:

- **Color Placement**: Use color to manipulate depth perception. The red colours give a perception of closeness and the colours purple and violet give the perception of things being further away. Plant red and warm-coloured flowers near the house and use cooler colors like purple and violet flowers farther from the house to give the illusion of distance and depth.
- **Curved Pathways**: Design pathways that are curved rather than straight. Curved paths create a perception of increased length, since the eye does not automatically see the end of the path.
- **Pathways Leading Beyond the Garden**: Create the illusion that your garden continues beyond its actual boundaries by designing paths that appear to carry on into the distance. End paths at garden gates or gaps in a hedge, that suggest that the path continues after the end of the garden.

By integrating these visual elements into your urban living space, you can create a sensory connection to nature, enhancing your environment with the natural sights and benefits of the outdoors, even in the heart of the city.

Conclusion

By integrating natural views and elements into urban spaces, you can create a sensory connection to nature that significantly enhances your well-being. From window gardens and indoor plants to vertical gardens, rooftop retreats, and strategic plant placement, these techniques help bring the soothing and expansive qualities of nature into the heart of the city.

Not only do these strategies improve the aesthetic appeal of your living space, but they also provide mental and emotional benefits, such as reduced stress, increased relaxation, and a greater sense of connection to the natural world.

Chapter 30. Taste

The sense of taste is a fundamental and intimate aspect of the human experience, deeply intertwined with our emotions, memories, and overall well-being. Taste allows us to enjoy food and drink, making eating a pleasurable and enriching experience. This sensory modality is crucial for human survival, development, and enjoyment.

The Journey of Taste: From Mouth to Brain

When we eat or drink, taste buds on our tongue and other parts of our mouth detect chemicals in the food and send signals to the brain. These signals travel along the gustatory nerve to the brain, where they are processed in the gustatory cortex. This intricate process happens almost instantaneously, allowing us to perceive a wide range of flavours.

The Five Primary Tastes

The human tongue can detect five primary tastes: sweet, salty, sour, bitter, and umami (savoury). Each of these tastes is associated with specific types of food and provides essential information about the food we eat:

- **Sweet**: Often associated with energy-rich foods, sweetness signals the presence of sugars and carbohydrates.
- **Salty**: Saltiness indicates the presence of essential electrolytes, which are crucial for bodily functions.
- **Sour**: Sourness can signal acidity, which may indicate fermentation or spoilage in foods.
- **Bitter**: Bitterness often serves as a warning sign for toxic or harmful substances.
- **Umami**: Umami, or savoury taste, is associated with amino acids and proteins, signalling the presence of nutritious and protein-rich foods.

While these primary tastes provide the basic framework for our sense of taste, the full complexity and richness of flavours come from the sense of smell.

The Role of Smell in Enhancing Taste

The sense of smell plays a crucial role in augmenting the taste experience. When we eat, volatile compounds in the food are released and travel to the olfactory receptors in the nose. This process, known as retro nasal olfaction, occurs when we chew and swallow food, allowing aromas to reach the olfactory receptors from the back of the throat.

The olfactory receptors detect these volatile compounds and send signals to the brain, where they are integrated with the signals from the taste buds. This combination of taste and smell creates the full flavour experience, allowing us to perceive a wide range of complex flavours beyond the basic tastes detected by the tongue.

For example, when you eat a ripe, juicy strawberry, your taste buds detect its sweetness and slight acidity, while your nose detects its aromatic compounds. The integration of these sensory inputs creates the rich, multifaceted flavour that we associate with strawberries.

The Challenge of Artificiality in Modern Food

In modern urban environments, the sense of taste is often challenged by the artificiality of our city food. Many foods today do not taste as natural as they did a hundred years ago. This change is due to several factors:

- **Industrial Agriculture**: The rise of industrial agriculture has led to the mass production of food. While this has increased food availability, it has also prioritized quantity over quality. Crops are often bred for higher yields, longer shelf life, and resistance to pests rather than flavour.

- **Genetic Modification and Selective Breeding**: Many fruits and vegetables, like apples, have been selectively bred or genetically modified to enhance certain traits, such as size, color, and shelf life. This often comes at the expense of flavour. An apple today might look perfect but lack the complex taste profile of an apple from a century ago.

- **Soil Depletion**: Modern farming practices, including the use of synthetic fertilizers and monocropping, have depleted soil nutrients. This nutrient depletion can affect the flavour of fruits and vegetables, as the soil no longer provides the same richness of minerals and organic compounds that contribute to taste.

- **Artificial Additives**: Processed foods are often laden with artificial flavours, colors, and preservatives designed to enhance taste and appearance. These additives can mask the natural flavours of ingredients, leading to a diminished appreciation for the genuine taste of whole foods.
- **Global Supply Chains**: The globalization of food supply chains means that many fruits and vegetables are harvested before they are fully ripe to withstand long transportation times. This practice can result in produce that lacks the full flavour development that occurs when it ripens naturally on the plant.

The Impact on Our Taste Experience

These changes have had a profound impact on our taste experience. Foods that were once rich in natural flavours are now often bland or artificially enhanced. This can lead to a disconnection from the true taste of food and a reliance on processed and artificially flavoured products to satisfy our taste buds.

Reconnecting with Natural Flavors

To reconnect with the natural flavours of food and enhance our sense of taste, consider the following practices:

- **Buy Local and Seasonal**: Purchase fruits and vegetables from local farmers' markets. Seasonal produce is more likely to be fresh, naturally ripened, and full of flavour.
- **Grow Your Own**: If possible, grow your own herbs, vegetables, and fruits. Home-grown produce can offer a richer taste experience as you control the growing conditions and harvest at peak ripeness.
- **Choose Heirloom Varieties**: Opt for heirloom varieties of fruits and vegetables, which are often grown for their superior taste rather than their appearance or shelf life.
- **Minimize Processed Foods**: Reduce your consumption of processed foods and focus on whole, natural ingredients. This can help you appreciate the true flavours of food.
- **Mindful Eating**: Practice mindful eating by paying close attention to the flavours, textures, and aromas of your food. This can enhance your appreciation for natural tastes and improve your overall eating experience.

Conclusion

The sense of taste, enhanced by the sense of smell, is a gateway to the world of flavours, a trigger for emotions, and a vital part of our daily existence. By understanding and appreciating the depth and richness of our gustatory experiences, and by taking steps to reconnect with natural flavours, we can enhance our connection to the world around us and to our own personal histories. In the following chapters, we will explore how you can create and enjoy rich, flavourful experiences in your urban environment, bringing the joy and comfort of taste into your everyday life.

Apple Trees; Kwitnace Jablonie (Wikimedia Commons)

Chapter 31. Rediscovering Authentic Flavors

Connecting to natural flavours in the city can significantly enhance your culinary experiences and bring a sense of authenticity and enjoyment to urban living. Despite the challenges posed by modern food production, there are various strategies to find and savour natural tastes even in an urban environment. Here are some practical steps to help you reconnect with natural flavours in the city:

Buy Local and Seasonal Produce

- **Benefits**: Local and seasonal produce is often fresher, tastier, and more nutrient-dense than items shipped from far away.
- **How to Use**: Visit farmers' markets or join a Community Supported Agriculture (CSA) program to buy fruits and vegetables that are in season and grown locally. These options often provide produce picked at peak ripeness, offering superior flavour.

Grow Your Own Herbs and Vegetables

- **Benefits**: Growing your own herbs and vegetables ensures you have access to the freshest ingredients and allows you to control the growing conditions.
- **How to Use**: Utilize balconies, windowsills, or community gardens to grow herbs like basil, mint, and rosemary, as well as vegetables like tomatoes, peppers, and lettuce. Even small spaces can yield a satisfying harvest.

Choose Heirloom Varieties

- **Benefits**: Heirloom fruits and vegetables are often selected for their rich flavours and unique characteristics rather than for commercial production traits.
- **How to Use**: When shopping for seeds or plants, look for heirloom varieties. At farmers' markets, ask vendors about heirloom options. Examples include heirloom tomatoes, which offer a diverse range of flavours and colors, and heritage apples with more complex taste profiles.

Minimize Processed Foods

- **Benefits**: Processed foods often contain artificial flavours and preservatives that can dull your palate over time.
- **How to Use**: Focus on whole foods and ingredients. Prepare meals from scratch using fresh produce, whole grains, and natural proteins. Avoid items with long ingredient lists and unfamiliar additives.

Visit Specialty Grocers and Ethnic Markets

- **Benefits**: Specialty grocers and ethnic markets often carry unique and high-quality ingredients that can elevate your culinary experience.
- **How to Use**: Explore markets that specialize in organic, gourmet, or ethnic foods. These stores often offer a wider variety of natural and artisanal products, such as fresh herbs, spices, and regional specialties.

Engage in Foraging (Safely)

- **Benefits**: Foraging allows you to find wild, natural ingredients that are often packed with flavour and nutrients.
- **How to Use**: Learn about local edible plants and mushrooms that can be safely foraged in urban parks and green spaces. Take guided foraging tours to ensure you identify and harvest plants correctly. Always follow local regulations and guidelines.

Practice Mindful Eating

- **Benefits**: Mindful eating helps you fully appreciate the flavours, textures, and aromas of your food, enhancing your overall eating experience.
- **How to Use**: Take time to savour each bite, paying attention to the taste and aroma. Eat slowly, and avoid distractions like television or smartphones. Reflect on the flavours and how they connect to your memories and emotions.

Creating a Natural Taste Oasis in the City

To maximize the benefits of natural tastes in an urban setting, consider creating a culinary oasis at home:

- **Herb Gardens**: Create a small herb garden in your kitchen or on your balcony. Fresh herbs like basil, cilantro, and thyme can add vibrant flavours to your dishes.

- **Vertical Gardens**: Utilize vertical space to grow a variety of vegetables and herbs. Vertical gardens are ideal for small spaces and can yield a surprising amount of produce.

- **Indoor Fruit Trees**: Consider growing dwarf fruit trees indoors or on your balcony. Citrus trees, figs, and even small apple trees can thrive in containers and provide fresh, flavourful fruit.

- **Home Cooking**: Dedicate time to cooking meals from scratch using fresh, natural ingredients. Experiment with new recipes and ingredients to expand your palate and discover new flavours.

Conclusion

By integrating these practices into your urban lifestyle, you can reconnect with natural flavours and enhance your sense of taste. Embracing local, fresh, and unprocessed foods allows you to experience the full richness and complexity of natural tastes, bringing joy and satisfaction to your culinary experiences. In the following chapters, we will explore specific recipes and techniques to help you make the most of the natural ingredients available to you, transforming your meals into a celebration of authentic, natural flavours.

Herb Garden; DALL E

Epilogue: Rediscovering Emotion

In our fast-paced, modern world, it's easy to get swept away by an endless array of tasks and distractions. We're often caught in a whirlwind of obligations, rushing from one thing to the next, driven by the constant pressure to achieve and excel. In this relentless pursuit of progress, we gradually lose touch with something crucial: our inner sensitivity and our innate ability to truly feel and connect with the world around us.

The State of Overwhelm

Modern life can often feel like a never-ending race. Every moment seems accounted for, and our schedules are packed to the brim, leaving little room for reflection or genuine connection. This ceaseless activity, while often seen as necessary, comes at a significant cost. We become so engrossed in what needs to be done that we forget to notice how we are doing. Our minds, burdened with worries and plans, overshadow our natural capacity to experience life deeply and meaningfully.

In this state of constant overwhelm, we lose touch with the simple joys and profound experiences that make life rich and fulfilling. The vibrant, emotional core of our being becomes clouded, replaced by a mechanical response to life's demands. We lose the ability to take pleasure in simple moments, to feel empathy for others, and to connect with our own emotions. In our rush to keep up with the world, we sacrifice the essence of what makes us human.

Nature's Call to Reconnect

Amid this chaos, nature offers a profound remedy. The natural world, with its steady rhythms and serene landscapes, invites us to slow down and rediscover our lost sensitivity. By immersing ourselves in nature, we can begin to heal the fragmentation caused by our hectic lives. The sound of a gentle stream, the rustling of leaves, or the warmth of the sun on our skin can ground us and bring us back to a state of mindful presence.

By embracing the beauty and simplicity of nature, we can restore balance and find a deeper sense of purpose and fulfilment.

Embracing the Moment

Let us challenge the notion that everything we do in our hurried lives is of utmost importance. Take a moment to reevaluate what truly matters. Are the tasks that consume our time and energy really as critical as we believe? By questioning these assumptions, we can free ourselves from the cycle of rushing and stress, making room for more meaningful and fulfilling experiences and relationships.

Conclusion

In the end, the path to wholeness lies in rediscovering our emotions and reconnecting with the natural world. By embracing the power of nature and the richness of our sensory experiences, we can heal the disconnection and fragmentation that modern life often imposes on us. This journey is about finding balance, honouring our true selves, and living with greater intention and presence.

Nature; DALL E

A Song of Healing

In days of yore, ages ancient,
In times of earth's pure splendour,
Humans lived with deep connection,
To the rhythms of the seasons,
To the cycles of nature.

In the fields they toiled and laboured,
Hands in soil, and hearts in harmony,
Gathered harvest with their neighbours,
Bread they baked with love and patience,
Felt the pulse of life's pure essence.

Then the age of iron and engines,
Brought to the world steely marvels,
Machines to till, to weave, to gather,
Made the cities grow and prosper,
Yet they severed bonds with nature,
Led us far from earth's embrace.

In the hustle, in the clamour,
Lost were we in webs of metal,
Machines surround us, guide our journey,
Cars and traffic lights and towers,
Computers, planes, and smartphones buzzing,
Build our roads and power homes,
But our souls are left to wander.

Feel the loss of ancient wisdom,
Feel the pull of past connections,
Machines, though grand, are non-human,
Lack the touch of warmth and caring,
As we blend with them, we falter,
Move away from true belonging.

Yet within the heart of nature,
Lies the path to our redemption,
In the forests, by the rivers,
On the mountains, through the meadows,
Nature waits with open silence,
Calls us back to find our wholeness.

Walk among the trees so stately,
Feel the earth beneath our footsteps,
Hear the song of birds at sunrise,
See the dance of leaves in sunlight,
Touch the bark of ancient giants,
Breathe the air, pure and healing.

Practice mindfulness in nature,
Find the peace within the stillness,
Let the streams wash away sorrow,
Let the winds uplift our spirit,
Watch the clouds and find our vision,

In the vastness, find our balance.

By the gentle glow of sunset,
In the quiet of the twilight,
Reflect on life, embrace our essence,
Shed the layers of distraction,
Heal the wounds of past transgressions,
In simplicity, find gratitude,
In solitude, discover presence.

As the stars adorn the night sky,
Feel the bond with all creation,
In the web of life, we're woven,
Threads of joy and love unbroken,
Through the gift of nature's healing,
Find the wholeness, find the pleasantness,
Nature's wisdom, ever flowing,
Leads us back to our true being.

Thus we journey through the ages,
With the earth our guide and teacher,
In the harmony of nature,
Find the path to our completeness,
From the ancient ways of living,
To the future of our dreaming,
Nature's gift of endless healing,
Brings us peace and understanding.

In the whisper of the willows,

In the chorus of the pine trees,

Hear the message ever-echoed,

Nature's call to hearts awakened,

Through the gift of nature's treasure,

Find the wholeness, find the joy,

Live in balance, live in wonder,

In the dance of life unbroken.

Willows and Pine Trees; rawpixel.com

Appendix: The Countryside Code

The Countryside Code is designed to help you enjoy the stunning beauty of the countryside while keeping it safe and pristine for everyone. Following its simple guidelines ensures that nature, wildlife, and other visitors can continue to thrive and enjoy the great outdoors.

Respect Other People

- **Be Considerate**: Think about how your actions might affect those who live and work in the countryside, as well as other visitors.
- **Be Polite and Thoughtful**: Close gates behind you, avoid blocking driveways, and be friendly and courteous to others you meet along the way.
- **Stick to Paths and Use Gates**: Keep to marked paths and use gates and stiles when crossing fences to help protect fields, crops, and the countryside landscape.

Protect the Natural Environment

- **Leave No Trace**: Take your litter home with you and avoid disturbing wildlife. Properly dispose of all waste to keep the countryside clean and safe.
- **Be Fire Safe**: Be cautious with campfires and BBQs, especially during dry periods. Always make sure fires are fully extinguished before leaving.
- **Stay on Trails**: Help protect wildlife habitats and prevent erosion by sticking to designated paths and trails.
- **Care for Plants and Trees**: Avoid damaging plants and trees, and take special care in protected areas.

Enjoy the Outdoors Responsibly

- **Plan and Prepare**: Check the weather, carry a map, and ensure you have the right clothing and equipment for your adventure.
- **Know Your Limits**: Choose activities and routes that match your fitness level and let someone know your plans.
- **Extinguish Flames Completely**: Ensure any fires or BBQs are fully out before you leave to prevent wildfires.

Keep Dogs Under Control

- **Lead Your Dog**: Keep your dog on a lead, especially around livestock and wildlife, to avoid any accidents or disturbances.
- **Clean Up After Your Dog**: Dispose of dog waste properly to maintain a clean and healthy environment for everyone.

Follow Signs and Advice

- **Respect Signs and Notices**: Follow instructions on signs and respect any restrictions such as seasonal closures or specific access limitations.
- **Listen to Local Guidance**: Take advice from local rangers and landowners to ensure you're following best practices.

Conclusion

By following the Countryside Code, you preserve the countryside's beauty and tranquillity. Your respect, care, and responsibility help maintain this wonderful environment, ensuring it remains a joy for everyone to visit.

Printed in Great Britain
by Amazon